MW01096341

ACTIVATING
THE COMMON
GOOD

Also by Peter Block

Confronting Our Freedom:
Leading a Culture of Chosen Accountability and Belonging,
coauthored with Peter Koestenbaum

An Other Kingdom:
Departing the Consumer Culture,
coauthored with Walter Brueggemann and John McKnight

The Abundant Community:
Awakening the Power of Families and Neighborhoods,
coauthored with John McKnight

Community:
The Structure of Belonging

The Answer to How Is Yes:
Acting on What Matters

The Flawless Consulting Fieldbook & Companion:
A Guide to Understanding Your Expertise,
with Andrea Markowitz and others

Freedom and Accountability at Work:
Applying Philosophic Insight to the Real World,
coauthored with Peter Koestenbaum

Stewardship:
Choosing Service over Self-Interest

The Empowered Manager:
Positive Political Skills at Work

Flawless Consulting:
A Guide to Getting Your Expertise Used

ACTIVATING THE COMMON GOOD

Reclaiming Control of Our Collective Well-Being

PETER BLOCK

Berrett–Koehler Publishers, Inc.

Berrett-Koehler Publishers, Inc.
1333 Broadway, Suite 1000
Oakland, CA 94612-1921
Tel: (510) 817-2277
Fax: (510) 817-2278
www.bkconnection.com

ORDERING INFORMATION

Quantity sales. Special discounts are available on quantity purchases by corporations, associations, and others. For details, contact the "Special Sales Department" at the Berrett-Koehler address above.

Individual sales. Berrett-Koehler publications are available through most bookstores. They can also be ordered directly from Berrett-Koehler: Tel: (800) 929-2929; Fax: (802) 864-7626; www.bkconnection.com.

Orders for college textbook / course adoption use. Please contact Berrett-Koehler: Tel: (800) 929-2929; Fax: (802) 864-7626.

Distributed to the U.S. trade and internationally by Penguin Random House Publisher Services.

Berrett-Koehler and the BK logo are registered trademarks of Berrett-Koehler Publishers, Inc.

PRINTED IN CANADA

Berrett-Koehler books are printed on long-lasting acid-free paper. When it is available, we choose paper that has been manufactured by environmentally responsible processes. These may include using trees grown in sustainable forests, incorporating recycled paper, minimizing chlorine in bleaching, or recycling the energy produced at the paper mill.

Library of Congress Cataloging-in-Publication Data
Names: Block, Peter, 1939– author.
Title: Activating the common good : reclaiming control of our collective well-being / Peter Block.
Description: First edition. | Oakland, CA : Berrett-Koehler Publishers, [2024] | Includes bibliographical references and index.
Identifiers: LCCN 2023022887 (print) | LCCN 2023022888 (ebook) | ISBN 9781523005963 (hardcover ; alk. paper) | ISBN 9781523005970 (pdf) | ISBN 9781523005987 (epub) | ISBN 9781523005994 (audio)
Subjects: LCSH: Cooperation. | Common good. | Social capital (Sociology) | Community development.
Classification: LCC HD2961 .B625 2024 (print) | LCC HD2961 (ebook) | DDC 334—dc23/eng/20230616
LC record available at https://lccn.loc.gov/2023022887
LC ebook record available at https://lccn.loc.gov/2023022888
First Edition

31 30 29 28 27 26 25 24 23 | 10 9 8 7 6 5 4 3 2 1

Book producer and text designer: BookMatters
Cover designer: Ashley Ingram

To John McKnight

The words and ideas of neighborhood, gifts, productive functions of citizens, the limits of institutions, and most of what is the foundation for this book I learned from John. Plus, most of the people who are bringing these ideas to life I met through John. He has been a light unto the world for many decades. We have traveled many places and given many talks together, where most times John opens with content and changes the world with his ideas, then I break people into small groups. I got the better side of the deal.

To Walter Brueggemann

Walter, an Old Testament scholar, has also opened worlds in his lifelong devotion to interpreting and bringing sacred stories of the Bible to all who read and listen. His studies have lifted into view unexpected and merely human parts of the Bible that have been overlooked in our selective way of seeking certainty and a comfortable story. His friendship, teaching, and writing gave me a memory of what it means to be a Jew. Something I had forgotten or never knew. I discovered it was me that was a slave to Pharaoh for four hundred years, and then got lost in the wilderness, half thinking that at least under Pharaoh life was predictable. Walter's prophecy gives us the insight that it is neighborliness found in unexpected places that sustains us in impossible times. Which is all this book is about.

Though the commons is everywhere, it is little noticed. For economists, it is a kind of inchoate mass that awaits the vivifying hand of the market to attain life. Forests are worthless until they become timber, just as quiet is worthless until it becomes advertising.

JONATHAN ROWE

Sidewalk contacts are the small change from which the wealth of public life may grow.

JANE JACOBS

The cultural ideals were the knight, the monk, the philosopher and then they were all superseded by the cultural ideal of the businessman.

ROBERT INCHAUSTI

Hannah Arendt, covering the Eichmann trial for *The New Yorker*, advanced the theory of the banality of evil. There was nothing particularly rotten about Eichmann: he was not a psychopath but merely a painfully average man who regarded the state-sponsored madness around him as normal and therefore never hesitated to partake in its crimes.

LIEL LEIBOVITZ

CONTENTS

We Are Not Divided

All of us, one way or another, are drawn to what is considered good for the earth, for the community, for the general well-being of all individuals. This can go under the idea called the common good, one dictionary definition being "the good, welfare, or prosperity of a community or country as a whole; common well-being; the public interest."[1]

Given the inherent appeal of caring for what we all hold in common, it is confounding why this concept is not more at the center of our day-to-day collective attention. The intent of this book is to do something about that. The challenge is that we are now enveloped by a dominant culture that treats what is in the interest of our common good as an afterthought or a subject of contention. Concerns about the sustainability of the environment, social justice, an economy that works for all, care for the vulnerable, and more appear to hold simply a minority appeal, albeit a passionate and powerfully invested minority.

The common good in modern society is not well served. We

continue to reinforce and sustain social inequity, an increasingly fragile environment, violence in word and deed, and a general uneasiness about the human project. The challenge explored in this book is to discover what more we can do to reinforce the efforts to bring about a shift in the dominant culture.

Most current efforts to support the common good take several forms of activism. These include policy debates and advocacy, protests, decades of accumulating evidence on the climate crisis, theories of a new economics, more legislation, stories and studies, winning political campaigns, and the hope that more development, research, and technology will create a better future for us all. We are betting on all of these efforts, each valuable but not making enough of a difference.

In addition to reformers, protesters, change agents, one kind of activism identified by Bill Moyer is citizen activism.[2] This is meant to include promoting positive values, voting, and attending local civic activities. We want to widen the meaning of citizen activism to include building trust with other citizens and local strangers in a way that brings our interests together, regardless of all the ways we might differ. Too many of us and our neighbors are passionate about making things better, but are reluctant to be called activists.

The intention here is to reach the point where the common good is the organizing principle and paradigm for our culture. We can accelerate this movement by briefly discussing how our thinking and dominant cultural narrative got to the point where something other than the common good captures our attention and energy. We want to define a shift in certain fields of interest. Fields like journalism, architecture, and religion that can more actively help normalize the common good as our culture's organizing paradigm. These fields can shift in ways that profoundly strengthen the common good by supporting citizens in reclaiming control over our collective well-being. This is a critical part of producing new ways of living together and resting lightly on the planet.

The common good as used here also speaks to our approach to several very specific and widely shared communal concerns. Based on more than forty years of research and practice, John McKnight and the Asset-Based Community Development Institute have found that what every community universally cares about is finding the best ways to collectively:

- Educate and raise our children

- Be healthy

- Protect the planet

- End the isolation of each of us and those most vulnerable

- Be safe

- Sustain a local livelihood

- Bring about social equity[3]

Each of these concerns is a world unto itself. Together they constitute measures of our individual and communal well-being. This book is for those people who are dissatisfied with the progress we are making in these areas of concern. It is for those who understand that even though *I* may be doing well, *we* aren't. For any one of us, some concerns will have greater priority over others.

For our discussion here, these communal concerns are held to be intertwined, dependent on each other, so that real change in any one area of concern cannot be satisfied without dramatic movement in all of them. The term *common good* is shorthand for this point of view. This book centers on the idea that one element of elevating the common good will occur by rebuilding the strength of local citizen accountability. This means reconsidering the shape of our activism and leadership, and increasingly putting our well-being more directly in the hands of citizens and their associational life.

This reconsideration of activism, which we call "relational activism," will take into account and support our existing efforts to change our institutions and so-called large systems. Relational activism begins with the thought that winning elections and acting as if we are defined by the actions of industry, government, foundations, and educational and service institutions is not working well enough. The way we habitually blame individuals in power for our condition is also not working. Big systems, their practices, and their point persons are major players, of course, and their support is welcomed at every step of the way, but it is useful to suspend the idea that they have the capacity to lead us into an alternative future.

The common good as developed here is a counternarrative to what we call the business perspective. The business perspective has a set of protocols good for commerce. And it is valuable in that way. The challenge is that we are trying to use its belief system to deal with all of our other concerns. The business perspective values growth, scale, speed, convenience, and predictability. This dominant cultural narrative celebrates competition and individualism. This view is based on the conviction that our future depends on a strong consumer culture and a global reach.

The business perspective and the common good will always coexist. The business perspective makes some contribution to the common good, but the two paradigms are distinct and separate. We need to stop believing that the business perspective can be used as a primary agent for activating the common good. The business perspective does aid the common good with its capital surplus and generosity. However, it does not have the capacity to make the common good a top priority.

To prioritize the common good over the business perspective is no small undertaking. To be sure, traditional activism has done amazing work in defining the common good. It has provided research and evidence and voice for the common good and created common good networks and alliances. This is all essential. This book explores new ways—initially ways of thinking rather than doing—that encourage more powerful responses to our collective areas of concern.

Our efforts toward activating the common good begin with making distinctions. Each belief system—the business perspective and the common good perspective—rests on a set of assumptions that constitute a narrative or paradigm about our culture, our habitual ways of being together, and what best serves society. One popular, well-publicized feature of the current dominant story is the idea that we are fundamentally divided and polarized as a society. This notion is treated as if it is true. The common good perspective declares that we are not fundamentally divided, which might mean that we are too passive in accepting the polarized storyline. The approach here is not about arguing which narrative is true. It is about deciding which narrative actually is *more useful.*

Which narrative is more useful in terms of how our children are doing? In terms of the local circulation of money and our collective measures of health? In terms of our sense of connection, our feeling of safety and evidence of equity, racial and otherwise? In the United States, where we think we are the greatest, we aren't. For all of our spending capacity, the country barely ranks in the top twenty in most measures of well-being. This includes health, safety, impact on the earth, and belonging.

Reclaiming Control of Our Collective Well-Being

Along with exploring the common good perspective, we need to give form and shape to the means by which citizens reclaim control of their well-being. As a consumer culture, we are in the habit of out-sourcing answers to our concerns. We are lulled into convenience and demand being well-serviced. It will take a special kind of activism and engagement for citizens to rediscover their sense of agency for what matters most. Part of the journey throughout this book is to be specific about ways to invite citizens to directly create and control what they care most about. To become citizens first and consumers on occasion.

Wherever you are, there exist examples of citizens who have in fact taken control of their communal concerns. There are churches bringing economic equity to their neighborhoods, residents working to keep youth out of the judicial system, citizens bringing safety to a city, groups improving their health by making their neighborhoods more habitable. Many more stories show that our shared concerns are being fulfilled by citizens in a given place, finding what they can create together.

The question arises, what is the nature of these innovations in citizen accountability and relational activism and how have they come into being? For one, this kind of citizen and community organizing does not count on the business perspective to address the concerns of the common good. Many of our efforts to advocate the common good try to influence the business perspective to bring about change. We are in the habit of targeting the people in charge, believing they can bring about reform or transformation. We focus on executives, elected officials, and institutional leaders, including social service providers, bankers, developers, and board members. Historically, we have believed that if we engage in more research and studies to better define the problems, we can better solve them. So, we invest in more visions and planning based on studies. We also want change to happen quickly and on a large scale, and we believe it requires major funding.

Of course, all of these well-meaning forms of action help and are worth doing. The question is whether these ways of thinking and doing are powerful enough to reach our destination. The problem is that our more dramatic efforts at activism have difficulty sustaining attention and most often evoke responses that are more cosmetic than authentic. For example, leadership will respond to protests but usually in a symbolic way, offering more training for managers and police. Naming diversity, equity, and inclusion vice presidents. Declaring war on poverty and a war on drugs. Setting ambitious goals with designated funding. Making public declarations and manifestos. Devising new measurements that have several bottom lines. Underwriting more research. Being active in managing the news.

The challenge is how to activate the common good in ways that enter our daily lives and keep people engaged once the issue is off the front page.

Relational Activism: Citizens Finding the Other

What is needed is local, relationship-based activism that endures over time and is less dependent on the transformation of people in the traditional leadership positions. This is where we must adopt new protocols for mobilizing the common good. Most ways of engaging citizens are cause-oriented gatherings and promotions. Progressive news sites. Events designed to convince and persuade and educate. They feature passionate speakers. Experts presenting research findings. Calls for action. Panels on stage. Dialogues or interviews with well-known experts. Presentations on what has worked elsewhere. These are the forms in which dominant change is attempted. Whether in person or virtually. Traditional forms of activism that enlist, recruit, inspire, and pressure others to change are variations of a marketing strategy. They are selling something, treating the audience as consumers. They are likely to inspire and excite in much the same ways that movies and the arts do. This approach is valuable but not transformational.

Suppose we decided that the purpose of bringing people together, whether in groups of five or five hundred, was to take advantage of the one irrefutable thing they have in common: *the fact they showed up.* Say we used each occasion to have them find each other. To have them trust each other—especially strangers—in a short period of time, say fifteen minutes. Suppose we used that connection to mobilize their energy to take actions over that which they have control. Let them sort themselves into groups by their interests. Ask those who would be willing to come to one more meeting to sign up and come back to focus on what they care most about and can control.

This way of bringing people together is different from education, persuasion, research, and good examples. We call this approach relational or convening activism. The main intent is to create social capital. It is a counterapproach to strategies that call for better management and leadership, and for someone else to change. It involves helping citizens to find each other and create relationships that produce something compelling to work on in addition to canvassing, sending money, and writing letters.

As relational activists, we focus on citizens' experiences with one another. We are thankfully in the habit of coming together for our common concerns about racism, schools, violence, and social justice. But on the question of action, something is needed to convert the consumer who came to listen and support into the citizen who leaves to produce.

For citizens and members of an association or activist group, we might focus more on building social capital in the moment. The idea is to have more people choose to come together and continue with those who might have been strangers. Social capital is built so people are more trusting and will work with others on an issue they have chosen and made a commitment to. We can construct every gathering with the primary purpose of fostering connection among peers. We know how to do this by the way we structure the time and choose the right questions to ask. This promotes equity in how we see one another. It is a form of relational activism where there is nothing to wait for.

The future exists in each moment. To this end, the activist convener uses a variety of ways to open worlds and sustain energy. Throughout the book we are specific about these methods, which we call common good protocols.

The Shape of the Common Good

Organizing our culture around the common good requires us to be willing to turn strangers into neighbors, and it is already occurring. All around us. This book is not about what *is* the common good, or the commons, or commoning, or where these efforts are working. That task has been spoken poetically again and again, most recently in *The Commoner's Catalog for Changemaking,* the Schumacher Center and David Bollier's amazing Whole Earth approach to describing the commons. If you want to know where the commons is working around the world and has been proven successful over years, read that book. Someday, *The Commoner's Catalog* will sit next to the Bible in hotel bedside tables.

Critical Fields of Interest

For the common good to become our dominant story, certain fields of interest are critical. They don't get the attention that the environment, social justice, and the economy receive, yet they are fundamental to creating conditions for the common good. These fields are journalism, architecture, religion, and the neighborhood. Seeing the shift possible in these domains is essential to ending the common good as being merely an alternative narrative. The business perspective is currently reinforced in each of these fields. For example, journalism is too often built on what is not working and who is at fault. Architecture tends to maximize economic return for each piece of land and reinforce our isolation. Religion has traditionally sought to convert citizens into its belief system. Modern neighborhoods are ranked on the price of real estate, the college admissions of their young residents, and upward mobility. Too many neighborhoods that don't get high rankings tend to export spending and are labeled for what is called the brokenness of low-income living.

The common good narrative needs to construct a counterdominant story in each of these fields. For instance, journalism could give first priority to what is working and end the obsession with what is not. Architecture could make secondary the economic value of land and could produce buildings, preserve open land, and create interior spaces in a way that brings people together. Religion holds the very language of the common good and can move into building community, regardless of beliefs. Neighborhoods are where citizenship and accountability for producing our well-being reside, where people's lives are much richer and more textured than can be expressed by their annual income.

These counternarratives are successfully occurring but most often as an alternative path. Without attention to reconstructing the dominant narrative of these chosen fields of interest and their need for each other, the common good will continue to be seen as simply an alternative. It is our challenge to expand these domains and bring them to the center of our attention. This begins the moment we collectively believe in the common good.

When I asked my friend Walter Brueggemann why it took the Jews four hundred years to leave Pharaoh's Egypt, he said they could not imagine being free. For the common good to become the dominant narrative for our world, we only have to imagine that we can experience, in our own place, within reach, the capacity to produce our own well-being. And give this our fullest attention. This becomes our version of freedom, revitalizing the productive functions of our neighborhood and community. That is our best way to care for ourselves and the planet. Getting there is a modern Red Sea crossing.

ONE

Taking Care of Business

Socialism never took root in America because the
poor see themselves not as an exploited proletariat
but as temporarily embarrassed millionaires.

JOHN STEINBECK

Our culture's current dominant narrative is named here as the business perspective. But it has to do with much more than commerce. The business perspective dominates the role and functioning of our major institutions: government, democracy, international relations, urban planning, real estate, social equity, and social services. This narrative also defines our culture and how we live together.

The term *business perspective* is useful because it does not blame anybody. It defines the structure and direction of such fields of interest as journalism, architecture, religion, neighborhood, and more. It sets the context for how we work on such common concerns as education, the environment, our health and safety, social equity, and our isolation. We have been looking for the business promise of better management, control, and blueprints to work in these areas of concern. The business perspective at its core is attracted to modernity, which is about what is new and what is next. This narrative requires proof of where something is working and asks, before anything else, how much does it cost, how long will it take, and is it replicable? These questions commodify us and keep the system in place, even though they promise transformation.

No Longer the Alternative

In the dominant narrative of the business perspective, concerns for what fully serves our well-being but has no commercial or political value are treated as exceptions and alternatives. Alternative health, alternative economy, alternative education, alternative journalism. As for concerns about racism and racial equity, mainstream thinking in this narrative funds training programs for diversity, inclusion, and equity rather than investing directly in the redistribution of land and valuing the human assets in all of our neighborhoods. We offer efforts at economic justice through Community Benefit Agreements, Opportunity Zones, and the Community Reinvestment Act. But these efforts are implemented in a way that is either lip service or widens wealth disparities.

We can no longer live by having what we value most considered an "alternative" world. Too many of us are weary of remaining human-interest stories in the local section of the news. Of being reported on only in crises. Of never being the lead story in the evening news, only a feel-good upbeat note before signing off.

Advocates for the common good are accused of being idealists. When we choose to affirm cooperation, and focus on people's gifts and what is collectively working, we are considered touchy-feely types, in contrast to realists. Reality is the selling point of commerce and cynicism. "Getting real" is always the argument that results in nothing shifting. "Realism" as it is used, however, rests on the belief that self-interest is who we are. So much of what constitutes this dominant business narrative, with Adam Smith as a major voice, declares that self-interest, materialism, and being competitive constitute "reality." Darwin reported on cooperation as the basis of evolution, yet what was extracted from his work was the survival of the fittest, namely the most competitive.

The storyline of self-interest is glorified and legitimized in the dominant narrative. But self-interest is "in reality" a social construction, another term for *fiction*. When we accept that each narrative—the business perspective or the common good—is another social construction, it creates the opening for a counterstory. The common good perspective sets aside self-interest as a core principle on which to base a culture and way of being together. It creates a story based on the possibility that we built to be connected.

Could this be true? Who knows? You choose which researcher to quote. Show me the brain science. Listen to your historian of choice. The premise here is that in caring for the domains of the common good, an alternative to the business narrative is likely to be more useful. For example, the realms of raising a child, education, health, care for the planet, and safety do not want to be run like a business. They are not successful when they are fundamentally considered problems to be solved. When youth are seen to need socialization, when health has to be delivered by experts, when the planet is waiting for improvement, and safety has to be professionally guaranteed. Yet that is what we are doing. Most of our efforts and theories of change and improvement call for these "businesses" to be "run" better.

The option is to explore the ragged landscape of the common

good, beginning with a brief look at the culturally dominant business perspective. The Magna Carta was a stance for the common good but was superseded by the modern story. This storyline of self-interest has been historically supported by the writings of Adam Smith, Garrett Hardin, Milton Friedman, and John Locke. It is embodied by the actions of European colonial exploits into Asia, Africa, and Latin America. By the western expansion of the United States including its attraction to low cost labor. By beliefs in Manifest Destiny, eminent domain, and the Doctrine of Discovery. The counterstory is to turn from all of this.

Note, however, that none of the concerns in this discussion are an argument against capitalism. Capitalism is not the problem. Nor is socialism an answer. Argument and opinion about either of these or more "isms" are interesting but take us nowhere in the moment. Also, the answer is not about more or less democracy. These debates are habits and keep us stuck. We have been mired in these arguments for a long time. It is the narrative of the dominant perspective that is in question. It is the business paradigm that needs to be contained, regardless of our governance or economic system. The work is to claim a wider version of the common good out of the warming ashes of where the business narrative has reached its limits.

Citizens Are the Point

A new pathway to restore the common good points to a dominant narrative that places our primary attention toward citizens and our capacity to control and produce solutions for what we are most concerned about. This is a storyline that brings together all the elements of the common good. Again, a dominant narrative is simply the story widely held to be true and one that claims to best serve society.

As we are interested in transforming this current narrative, the first step is to look closely at it to see how dominant it really is. To look at how, like an addiction or a habit, this perspective invades not only our thinking but also our thinking *about* our thinking. This paradigm cannot be changed through willpower, more science, or better problem solving. It has to be seen for what it is and accepted for how pervasive it is. All with clarity and minimum judgment. Only then is an opening created for a counternarrative to emerge and be chosen. This is why we must first explore a brief history and description of the business perspective.

The business perspective is organized on the belief that our well-being is improved when we seek more control, predictability, scale, and efficiency. Often packaged as improvement and development and more jobs. This is the heart of it. The idea that these values are working well is strongly promoted in our culture. The corollary is that the business perspective prospers when we are divided and longing for more. Our isolation makes us more vulnerable and easier to control, cheaper to hire, and more eager to yield to the authoritarian offer of certainty and the consumptive illusion that satisfaction can be purchased, with grades as a school child, income and upward mobility as an adult, chemistry in old age.

In our culture's dominant business perspective, we are guided by a narrative of scarcity and the belief that we are incomplete and need improvement. This narrative claims that there is not enough to go around, and that if you have too little, it is your own fault. So, to compete successfully in a scarcity world, you also need to be wary of the stranger, because the stranger stands in the way of getting what we want. This perspective calls for us to compete against other nations. This is the business case for the STEM curriculum in our schools, giving priority to science, technology, engineering, and math often at the expense of arts, humanities, and making things. It was assumed to be in our national interest to be the first to place a person on the moon. And to be shamed that we were not the first nation to place a person in space. The business narrative has expanded way beyond business (where it belongs)

Wendell Berry writes in *What Matters? Economics for a Renewed Commonwealth* about the flaws in our modern economy—increasing poverty, fragile families, environmental damage, rising health-care costs, and wealth disparity. These forms of suffering *do* get some attention in the business context. There are constant efforts at reform. Reform does not address the narrative, however—the thinking underlying what drives the suffering. Instead, solutions such as more schooling, more efficiency, technology in every hand reinforce the faith that we should keep trying harder to solve problems so that we can keep our perspective.

The commitment to speed, cost, and convenience replaces people. Berry asks what to do with these replaced people. He answers the question by saying that "replaced people have entered into a condition officially euphemized as 'mobility.'"[4] So, in addition to modern problems of land, waste, and pollution, we have the problem of displacement. Displacement began in the 1600s with enclosure. The machine then came along and drew people to wage labor and the city. Digital processes now automate our being together, and artificial intelligence is already writing poetry for us and doing our homework.

But this is not a case against technology. Or against speed, cost, and scale—they are useful. The wheel, printing press, electricity, the telephone, science and engineering bring important benefits. But just because something is amazing does not mean it must define us.

In addition to the efficiency and convenience of technology, the business perspective tends to define the many efforts to repair the side effects Berry mentions. We debate to seek adjustments in the distribution of capital: guaranteed annual wage, cap-and-trade emission systems, debt forgiveness, more health care, more public and affordable housing, earlier schooling, more policing, more minorities in top management, citizen review boards to exercise more control.

These are all efforts to redeem us from the liabilities of the current dominant narrative. They hope to make the business perspective work somewhat better. Perhaps. But these efforts are simply more of what we have been trying. None will shift us to the common good as an organizing principle. None really give citizens a path to seeing their gifts or experiencing greater control over what they care most about. Which is the essence of the common good.

No snowflake in an avalanche ever feels responsible.

THOMAS WOLFE

TWO

The Common Good Perspective

This, then, is the great humanistic and
historical task of the oppressed: to liberate
themselves and their oppressors as well.

PAULO FREIRE

A different narrative is needed to serve our common interests, one that holds that, regardless of our politics or religion or preferences and likes, there are interests that bind us together. Plus, there are ways to pursue these interests that make a bigger difference than what we are accustomed to. That recognize that welcoming the stranger, which is at the core of much of what separates us, is in our best interest.

This pursuit begins by understanding that our well-being cannot be purchased or healed by more professionals or programs. And that what we have and what we are is enough. Economically. Politically. Socially. Personally. This is the foundation of the common good narrative. It also chooses local and unique over scale and replicability. It replaces speed and convenience with slow and inefficient. It diverts attention away from who is in a leadership position, who occupies the front office. The common good narrative offers us an accessible path toward health, economic and racial equity, and rethinking how to respond to the unease and violence that is a part of life. This way of thinking is actually all around us but rendered invisible by practices in the core fields of interest such as journalism, architecture, religion, and the neighborhood.

To be more specific, we need to make the common good more newsworthy by supporting emerging *new journalism,* where our attention is drawn away from the front office and toward what works in local places. We need to affirm the impact occurring where *religious communities,* which hold the language of compassion and right relationships, are bringing together citizens outside their property lines, and are dedicated to investing in local residents, instead of servicing them. Where architecture holds a quality of aliveness and serves the community's social fabric instead of serving modernity and investors; where pocket neighborhoods, cohousing, hip-hop architecture, building design, and interior spaces all carry the message of collective and communal agency and connection. Where the neighborhood is a place where strong social relations can produce local livelihood, safety, and collective child-raising capacities. And finally, where an economics of enough, not scarcity, rests in local hands. This means that measures of well-being and wealth are not about money or possessions but about people benefiting from strong social capital; we trust those around us and work together; to make the place better. The point is, we can cooperate in pursuit of the common good in these fields, even when we see the world differently, which should be the least of our concerns.

Moving toward the common good questions the conventional belief that our narrative, or story, is produced by our history. That, as individuals, we are destined to be a product of our family, our genetics, life events, or even zip code. This cause-and-effect version of who we are is nurtured by the dominant narrative of business perspective as it strives to explain and justify itself. In the world of anthropology, sociology, psychology, and history, there is too little recognition that the eyes that are bearing witness are actually producing what they think they see.

This is not to discount the reality of facts and science. We need some control and scale and predictability. A chair has a certain shape and serves a certain function. In the world of beliefs and worldviews, however, it is useful to consider that the eyes have it. This idea is not offered as a debate about nature or nurture or free will or what is right or wrong. Rather, it is offered as a way of thinking about narrative and context as openings to new possibilities instead of as windows that remain closed and futures that are inevitable when we hold onto our conventional narrative, the business perspective. The counternarrative, the common good perspective, may not be true, and it has its own liabilities, but it might be useful.

Producers of the Common Good

The aspect of the common good perspective explored here is focused on the belief that we can produce rather than purchase our wellbeing. This thinking is at the core of the counterstory. This is the essence of an activated common good movement: that citizen-leaders can and are inventing ways for themselves and their neighbors to be safe, produce a local and inclusive economy, produce good health, produce and distribute a secure and local food supply, care for people on the margin, live out social justice, care for the land, and do a better job of raising children, especially if they are not ours. These are the outcomes and right measures of our well-being.

Citizens committed to these efforts through engagement with each other are the producers of the common good. They are not acknowledged by typical measures of annual income, educational level, or safety statistics for a place. Existing measures such as consumer spending, automotive sales, and the cost-of-living index tell us nothing important about our lives. They are very recent devices to measure economic success.

The free-market economy sustains its power because we can't imagine *not* being consumers. I can't imagine being a citizen. I can't imagine being enough. All the language about the knowledge economy is really about convenience, digital execution, and a set of virtual relationships. One step toward a communal economy is to let the knowledge and consumer economies return to where they belong and began—well done, valuable, and mildly interesting.

A communal economy would mean restoring the dignity of subsistence living. Called by some the "vernacular" world, it has the memory and resources that make life workable. We would acknowledge that the unpaid economy is truly what sustains us. Some call it an economy of generosity. And there are places that are measuring this. We just never consider it news or important. In an indigenous and truly sustainable economy, we care about small and unique, not scale. Walking distance, not global reach. Kindness to the soil, not cost and logistics, or patenting a seed.

The common good narrative creates space for another place to put our attention: the neighbor and community who have historically welcomed each other as well as the stranger. The amazing unpaid economy that has been quietly serving the common good for centuries and decades has laid the groundwork for this shift in attention. This narrative sees humans as something other than their financial or living condition, especially the people whom we label as "marginal" or "disadvantaged." Or "underdeveloped." Or "poor." There is no such thing as a marginal or disadvantaged or poor person. There is no such thing as an underdeveloped country.

Impacting the Future

Transformation is a shift in story or context or narrative. The shift to the common good as the dominant perspective begins by this naming of our choice of narrative. In the beginning was the word. The new word or narrative begins with a shift away from modernity and the societal value of newness, consumption, convenience, and growth. Call it a neighborly narrative, one interested in a movement from wealth as money to wealth as collective well-being. It is only recently that we have equated wealth with money. How do we move toward a new belief system?

It requires we go deeper into our existing collective narrative. To see that each ingrained feature of our narrative—such as our passion for development, mobility, and modernity—is actually a social construction. The current dominant narrative began in seventeenth century England. Enclosure, where public land was fenced in for private profit, was a dramatic contemporary shift away from the idea of the commons. This shift eventually celebrated progress, which became the rationalization for the Industrial Revolution. Fencing in land led to celebrating the machine, the extraction of resources in Africa, and the institution of slavery and westward expansion in America.

Those of us who protest capitalism and individualized greed—easy targets within the dominant narrative—blame those at the top. Reformers and revolutionaries who want the top to revise itself give as much attention to the importance of those in authority as those who defend it. The arguments about capitalism, socialism, communism, libertarianism, left and right, all still treat the top, executives in and out of government, as the source of the problem and the solution. They are seen as the key actors who are decisive in our well-being. While we may prefer to have certain people at the top, or want other systems of organizing the top, the actions of the top are rarely decisive. And they come and go with the tides of the times and nothing changes as long as the progress narrative stays the same.

What would constitute change is a shift in our thinking and where we put our attention. Seeing people as enough, skilled and learned, regardless of schooling. Deciding to measure communal social capital rather than the accumulation of financial capital or income. Some examples are described in words from Jonathan Rowe: "A better-protected commons would restore opportunities for interaction in daily life. The commons would encourage cities and suburbs with houses built close together, porches for visiting, and shops within walking distance. It would encourage mixed uses and granny flats instead of malls and sprawl and would build common spaces."[5]

There is the opportunity for expanding the common good with what exists in most neighborhoods. The buildings for supporting the common good are in place. The library. Mosques, temples, and churches. The museum. The grange hall. The hardware store. Coffee shops. The fire station. The neighborhood school after classes. Plus pavilions, parks, walkways, and bike trails. We need to find unique ways to more fully occupy these spaces and treat that as newsworthy.

As a pathway to fundamental shifts toward belonging and our common good, regular citizens become the center of our attention. We see them as citizens, not customers or voters. It is time for a wide range of citizens to become relationship-focused activists that capture and provide form to a counterstory to the current dominant business narrative. This is turning away from the ideas of progress, industrialization, the Information Age, and fencing me in. The effort to enter a counternarrative of the common good becomes a mixture of memory, art, and imagination through which we come to realize that we have the possibility to reconstruct an economy, our land use and architecture, our journalism, and our faith communities, and to create neighborhoods that are whole and represent a world that we are proud to inhabit and pass on as owners, limitations included.

The common good perspective calls for us to make citizen belonging, agency, and accountability the prime objective of our community-serving institutions. Their expertise in health, education, social service, and public service always remains important. It is the tone and culture of how these institutions engage those they serve that is in question. In each case this would entail focusing on people's gifts. Using groups of peers to sustain learning and citizens to create accountability. Working with citizens as partners and coproducers, not as customers. Schools based on peer-to-peer learning. Then offer institutional expertise to be of service.

The common good shifts our thinking about the quality of life. It values land for its own sake and nature for its aesthetics, vitality,

and potential to inform us about aliveness and harmony in its cycles of life, death, and seasons. The common good narrative believes
that livelihood can occur in a way that does not extract money from
local neighborhoods, or irreplaceable substances from the earth. It
encourages citizens to be primary players in educating a child and
keeping a neighborhood safe, and recognizes the value of caring
about land and its people over time. The common good keeps the
market in perspective. The market is a valuable creator of products
and exchange but not our central organizing principle.

There are many efforts in support of this kind of commitment and
understanding, and many examples are mentioned throughout this
book. The challenge is to elevate the common good to take priority
over our wish for streets paved with gold and our romance with the
miracle of science and technology. The common good is about neighborhood collective action stamped with the romance and magic of
human connection. The key is to operate in cooperation with the machine and the chip. To work in cooperation with them, but not yield
to an algorithm, a digital cloud, an artificial intelligence, a virtual-
reality glimpse of our culture and world.

Leaders and Activists as Conveners

This counternarrative includes the belief that the ways we physically
and operationally come together are transformational elements un-
dervalued in modernist culture—the room itself, how we organize
our gatherings, the questions we ask, all of which constitute how we
find each other in the midst of what we care most about. A piece of
this is called belonging and is much more than an affinity for a place

or a set of people. Belonging is a shared belief that we have enough in common and enough gifts to create together a life we want to live without waiting for change at a distance. This way of thinking and being is foundational to any hope for a different future. The idea is that a lateral and horizontal focus, with citizens and peers at its center, will allow our common concerns to be more fulfilled in the world. This could be considered relational activism, the politics of peers. The notion of leaders and activists as conveners is built on the belief that it is not decisive who occupies the front office or how much expertise is delivered.

As we choose to have the common good become the dominant narrative of our world, there are particular aspects of transformation that are important to grasp. Transformation does not occur until we can accept without judgment the context we have historically, culturally, and personally occupied. What is required is the searing knowledge of the nature of our participation and accountability in the business perspective. Transformation begins when we accept our history as we have constructed it.

This acceptance, and seeing our role within that narrative, creates the condition for naming and choosing a different future—in this case the common good. It does not make that future more "real" or true; it only names a future that opens possibility and provides a starting point for restoring our humanity and its capacity to fulfill our deepest concerns. Transformation comes with naming our own version of a future we are willing to construct and choose to inhabit. This is where freedom and accountability intersect.

All that follows here is based on this notion of transformation. It defines the kind of relational activism that holds the means to connect people who would never consider themselves activists. It calls us to different ways of coming together or convening as a form of activism, where activism works to produce a future without waiting for anyone else to change. The work is to engage neighbors in what they care most about and provide an experience for them where, from their willingness to belong, they choose to produce the well-being they desire and realize they do not have to purchase it. The focus is on convening that is organized around questions that accelerate trust among citizens as activists. This approach integrates relationships and purpose. The structure of the questions and how the room is configured facilitate trust and cocreation, creating a new context, in this moment. Each time we are engaged with each other in a unique and intimate way, the future is occurring, now.

This is not about how we hold a meeting, although it can seem that way. It is about how we come together other than what has become normal within the business perspective. Each time we gather, regardless of the numbers, begins our approach to transformation. Step one is always a conversational shift. Having a different conversation from those we are accustomed to, often with people we are not used to talking to. This movement occurs in a form to give voice to and amplify a new story of the power of what is neighborly and local in the face of the existing context of business, and its perspective, as usual.

To offer a simple example of shifting the conversation in order to shift the context, we decide to avoid the typical question-and-answer section of a gathering. The question-and-answer format only reinforces the idea that citizens have questions and experts and leaders have answers. Instead, we break the people in the room into groups of three and ask them to answer this question: "What is the crossroads you are at with respect to the subject we have gathered for?"

It's a simple question, but it is a metaphor for relocating where the source of possible action will come from. The content of the question calls for each citizen, in this moment at least, to act as one who has a choice. This is a glimpse of transformation, and this is how a new narrative is constructed, in small moments and peripheral vision.

We Have All the Evidence We Need

In every community, in every field of interest, there are people living the counterstory of the common good. Care for the commons goes under a variety of names. Walking school bus, creating local currencies, local business associations, improving the circulation of money. It is also called eliminating honeysuckle, creating bike lanes, designing low-income housing that produces wealth for its residents. It is planting vegetables and flowers in urban spaces; engaging the economically isolated; and ending racial inequity. Care for the commons looks like urban farming, book clubs, access for all to health. It is welcoming new citizens into schools and the YWCA commitment to a more racially equitable community and better life for women. This is the foundation for the potential dominance of the common good perspective.

One example of where the counternarrative now exists in our communities is Edgar Cahn's TimeBank concept, a technology-assisted structure that creates a means for tracking reciprocity among neighbors. TimeBanking uses time rather than money as a currency, and every person's time is of equal value. This approach connects individuals through their relationships and generosity, not through their credentials or their financial situation. Give one hour of service in a multitude of possible areas (for example, eldercare, barbering, shopping, home care, legal services), receive back one "time" credit that can be used to receive services. In human service endeavors the TimeBank helps people on the receiving end, those we once called people with needs, realize that others need what they also can provide. People are called coproducers.

TimeBanking now exists in forty countries. Edgar explains the concept: "Much of what has been done that we are really proud of as a culture is not about money. It's about engagement as neighbors and a kind of extended family. And so I thought that we need to find a currency, create a currency, that begins to reward that. We have not understood how vast the capacity is in a community that can produce our well-being without money."[6] TimeBanking, along with other social inventions, supports a core economy that acts in parallel to the monetary economy. It is a very buildable way for every neighborhood to reclaim control of its well-being.

We Are the Economy

A cornerstone of modern economics is the belief that the private sector offers the best ownership and management for the general well-being. The alternative to privatization is not necessarily to put these concerns into the hands of government or the sectors of society that have the word *social* in their name. Social service. Social work. Social entrepreneurship. Socialism. The alternative to privatization is to say that citizens, in a given place, can find the best mix of citizen initiative, communal ownership, and system support to care for those things that mean the most to us, such as land, health, and housing.

Reaching this possibility involves a kind of activism that supports and yet might be more powerful than protesting against or lobbying and persuading those seemingly in charge. The alternative to privatization or social services is to focus on citizens who can produce our collective well-being. This is not nostalgia or the wish to go back. It does call for memory of what matters. The "systemic change" we seek may lie in our own hands. Perhaps we are the system we came to change.

When we ask our children what grade they got, or tell our friends about our children's wins on the field or their upward mobility, we are quiet participants in promoting the business perspective. Our children's accomplishments are not in question here; it is that we let achievements on the career path define who they are, just as we label those on the margins as being poor and broken. This is our participation in sustaining the scarcity, speed, and scale economy.

A simple example is how the business perspective shapes education. The school has become the delivery system for commercializing the person through competition. The bell curve converts learning into performance. For school, the child is the product, the grade is the currency, employment is the purpose. Contrast that with this view from former First Lady of Ohio, Frances Strickland, who says that her goal for education is that every eighteen-year-old in the state knows what they are good at. This calls for students to think of themselves as something more than class rankings, awards, or advancement.

With the common good narrative as context, many schools now give more choice to the parent and child as to how the student learns best. Grades are de-emphasized. Some classrooms have students in small groups helping each other learn. In this way students share their gifts with each other. Also, rebellious or aggressive behavior is referred to students and teachers trained in mediation and restorative practices, which keeps the child within the school circle instead of being isolated and shamed through suspension. Belonging receives as much attention as achievement. And this is happening right now. We have the proof of concept in school systems around the country. All that is required is that each of our communities becomes interested in this model. And we as adults let go of our affection for blue ribbons.

Summing Up

The common good perspective has a bias toward neighbors reclaiming the core functions of right livelihood, which is making a living in a way that is restorative to what it touches. The common good recognizes that our health is in our own hands. It affirms that we have enough and we are enough, regardless of our credentials and income. And it reclaims more control of the land and the development process. This can reverse the process of enclosure that launched the business perspective centuries ago and still occurs today under the guise of eminent domain and economic development.

A lot of people mistake a short memory for a clear conscience.

DOUG LARSON

THREE

The Business Perspective

Every time you add a lane, you slow down traffic 4 mph.

BRAESS'S PARADOX ABOUT INTERSTATE HIGHWAYS

The more we see clearly the history and presence of the business perspective, and accept it for what it is, the more likely we can grow a counternarrative of the common good. The business narrative in its modern form did not emerge naturally by evolution, or as an inevitable shift away from communal practice or preference. While it first took form in the seventeenth century with enclosure, and was advanced by the machine and the Industrial Revolution, its current dominance was a product of post–World War II opportunism and a new aspect of the narrative: the free-market consumer culture. One event symbolizes what led to the expansion of the interstate highway system, the growth of the suburbs, and the standard of a chicken in every pot and a car in every garage. All ingredients of the American Dream.

One Origin Story

The origin of the free-market consumer culture can be traced to a meeting just after World War II. That meeting is precisely described in a report to the Club of Rome, by Hunter Lovins and her colleagues, called *A Finer Future: Creating an Economy in Service to Life.* Understanding the economic assumptions underlying this meeting makes clear the basis of the inequity, separation, and fear of the stranger that floods today's world. And pins it to a moment in time. *A Finer Future* describes this moment:

> The economic system that has brought us to the brink was made by men, 36 of them to be precise, who met in 1947. In the wake of a devastating world war, they set out to frame the economic system that they believed would deliver prosperity. Ludwig von Mises, Friedrich von Hayek, Milton Friedman and 33 of their intellectual associates met for ten days in Switzerland. The ideology they built, which they called neoliberalism, now underpins essentially all national economic policies... [they] championed the freedom of the individual to make economic decisions. They laid out their belief that government interference in economics was unmitigated evil, that there should be no meddling by government in individuals' choices. Strong property rights and free trade, they argued, are the best institutional means through which to achieve liberty and freedom....The Mont Pelerin Society they founded worked with the newly created Nobel Prize for Economics to get eight of its members chosen as winners and named as advisors to essentially every head of state on the planet. Three of them became heads of state and others central bankers.[7]

What have become the dominant, taken-for-granted market assumptions popularized by this gathering are captured very simply in the same book. Here is how Lovins and colleagues summarize the principles of our current dominant economic narrative:

We can have infinite growth on a finite planet.

Markets are the fairest form of exchange of things.

Prices tell the truth when unencumbered by government.

More income equals more happiness.[8]

These principles are the drivers of our dominant contemporary consumer culture as well as the worlds of finance, banking, global markets, and real estate. They form the core curriculum of almost every school of business. They are the liturgy of the *Wall Street Journal*, *The Economist*, the business sections of the *New York Times*, the *Washington Post*, Fox, Gannett, and most every other news agency. These principles give exclusive attention to stories about people in charge. Both their successes and failures. More about this later. They reinforce the importance of the consumer culture and the stock market as the primary measure of our economy, our democracy, and our well-being.

Capitalism

Ellen Meiskins Wood speaks of the power of capitalism as a system of exchange and as a way of life. Her book *The Origin of Capitalism* describes the dominant interpretations of capitalism. Capitalism is not the problem, she writes, it is our version that is in question: "Capitalism is a system in which goods and services, down to the most basic necessities of life, are produced for profitable exchange, where even human labour-power is a commodity for sale in the market, and where all economic actors are dependent on the market."[9]

This is the essence of what underlies the dominant narrative. It becomes the prevailing social construction when we consider it as a rule of life. When we believe that the market sits at the center of our existence. Again, the point is not to be for or against capitalism. It is that the business narrative is applied to every aspect of our lives, much more broadly than to the market. It holds for how all elements of society function: the environment, churches, early and higher education, health care, judicial systems, public works, philanthropy, politics, and social services. Even our ways of raising our children and caring for the elderly.

We have a choice about this. The capitalist structure is simply a way of moving and growing capital. It is mute on the purpose or use of the capital transfer it facilitates. The structure does encourage the private use of public money and land development, justified as a source of more gross tax revenue and more jobs. We have a choice about this also. More from Wood: "Because human beings and nature—in the form of labour and land—are treated, however fictitiously, as commodities in a self-regulating system of markets driven by the price mechanism, society itself becomes an 'adjunct' of the market. A market *economy* can exist only in a 'market society,' that is, a society where, instead of an economy embedded in social relations, social relations are embedded in the economy."[10]

The Consumer Culture

The business perspective in the contemporary world is intertwined with the so-called free-market consumer economy. Consumption in these terms is the core belief that without growth and scale and more, life is unsustainable. Whatever we have is not enough—regardless, and especially, if you have a lot. The business perspective and the consumer culture ballooned in the two decades after World War II: "What had become luxuries in the era before the Second World War now became necessities: refrigerators, clothes washers, telephones and record players....For the first time in history, 'leisure' became a problem. Average citizens could live as only the wealthy had lived in their parents' day (except that the personal servants who had performed routine tasks in wealthy homes were replaced by electrical appliances)."[11]

It is important to note that the consumer culture is about much more than shopping. Consumer culture promises that we can buy whatever we need. What is less spoken, however, is that the scarcity mindset that underpins consumer culture leads to what Walter Brueggemann calls Pharoah Logic: "From scarcity to accumulation to restless productivity to policy to priestly blessing to violence. This is how the consumer economy is the seed of violence."[12]

The business perspective is sustained by the measures we consider important. This becomes our order of worship, an organized and oft repeated sacrament. Some of the most popular measures of our market society are known as gross domestic product, standard of living, home ownership percentages, average annual income, unemployment rates, new job creation, consumer spending, new housing starts, social media likes and followers, and our famous neighbor, Dow Jones.

Technology and science are also major players and delivery systems for the consumer society. Consumer technology is designed for obsolescence. When you purchase a new cell phone or digital device, you need a newer one as soon as you walk out of the store or it arrives at your front door. There was a time when a telephone lasted a decade. Now it lasts a few months.

The question is not whether one uses or abstains from technology, but whether that technology, taken in the broadest context and longest run, is benign or serves as a substitute for social capital. The recurring question here is the extent to which what is most dear to us—such as raising a child, being safe, being healthy—remains under our capacity to produce. Online and social media connections are useful and entertaining. Surveillance systems help. Pharmaceuticals help. They can aid the common good but not produce it. Something more is needed for the well-being of the citizen, the community, and the culture at large.

A particular major period involving technology is worth special note. Kirkpatrick Sale has an interesting take on the impact of the Industrial era, which began with the invention of the steam engine. It became:

> The first manufacturing technology in human history that was, in a sense, *independent* of nature, of geography and season and weather, of sun or wind or water or human or animal power. It allowed humans for the first time…to have an instant unfailing source of power at their command….And thus it permitted the extraordinary shift from what had been an organic economy based on land and labor and local exchange to a mechanical economy based on fuel and factory and foreign trade, an empowerment of the machine in human society such as had never before been attempted.

It also led...to social and political consequences: squeezing
of farm populations and uncontrollable growth of cities,...the
enlargement of central governments, the enthronement of
science as ruling ideology.[13]

To summarize, the business perspective cuts a wide path. It serves
to make higher education essential, a side effect of which led toward privatizing debt which often turns out to be unrepayable. This
narrative runs on tax benefits to major industries, a practice that
is excluded from the discussion of smaller government. In organizations it takes the form of management, which is about order and
predictability. In schools it justifies the curriculum of job prepara-
tion. In communities it results in the dominance of the real estate,
insurance, banking, and finance industries, which are explained as
necessary for development. The business perspective leverages and
promotes real estate displacement, which moves low-income people
out of their traditional neighborhoods.

We are collectively aware of some of the limitations of this dominant perspective, which lead to attempts at reform that make little
difference. For a specific example, take health-care reform. We act
as if health is about lower costs, more technology, and more management. Every doctor we go to spends their time looking at a laptop,
not at a patient. Several years after investing $8.4 billion in putting
health-care records on computers, it turns out there was no impact
on health-care outcomes. The United States spends more than 50
percent more on health care as a percentage of GDP than the second biggest spender, Switzerland, yet has the lowest life expectancy
at birth, the highest death rates for avoidable or treatable conditions,

the highest maternal and infant mortality, and the highest rate of people with multiple chronic conditions.[14] Still, we claim we have the best health-care system in the world.

Bottom-Up Does Not Change Anything

Another example of being stuck in the business perspective is in the language of moving from a top-down way of working to a bottom-up way of working. Bottom-up has its appeal but still maintains the belief that the actions of the top are central to our thinking and needed to imagine and create a better future. The top is the desired destination. Bottom-up, which often goes under labels such as participatory management, civic engagement, citizen input, and citizen-based budgeting, does make the system more human and palatable.

All these approaches have value, so this is not an argument against more participation. But they do not change the belief that if you are seeking something truly different, it won't come from people in charge, no matter how hard they listen to those at the bottom. Transformation will not come from people at the bottom working harder to influence people at the top, or to *become* the people at the top. Engaging "the bottom" does make things somewhat better, but this is too small a god to worship. Also, it is a little strange that we call people, citizens, and employees "the bottom."

This all contributes to a world that believes that upward mobility is a universal measure of success. It begins in the first grade with the introduction of grades. The bell-shaped curve takes over; we accept a framework that introduces competition as the natural state of affairs and the key to learning. It rests on the belief that the student needs incentives to be motivated. Of course, I want to know how I am doing, and that I can learn more, but there are many ways to get that without ranking me against others. From the classroom we believe that employees need to be externally motivated and compete with each other. We love to rank everything. Schools, hospitals, countries, neighborhoods, restaurants, and more. This divides us by design. This journey from bottom to top tells us that we can always be improved and that people above and around us know what is best for us.

It Is Not from Lack of Effort

What gives impetus to shifting our perspective is the widespread knowledge that even those inside our institutions know something is not working. Many in education, health care, social service, and public service are frustrated with their own system and feel discouraged about anything really changing.

The challenge is to think beyond the reform being attempted. Most reform is about cost, technology, consistency, and control. Government reform is about less government. The safety discussion is about more police and better weapons, surveillance, strike forces, and technology. Education reform is about universal standardized curriculums spelled out by the state, more testing, and more executives and retired military running our schools. Financial reform is about more privatization of loans, and tighter regulation, or not. Unfortunately, many of these approaches have become politicized, which makes transformation even more difficult.

Simply declaring all of this to be a business narrative does not stop it. The intent is that it opens the opportunity for us to put a period on our belief in it. Just because something is compelling does not mean it needs to be all important or to define the nature of a way of life. Our goal is to place the business perspective where it rightfully belongs.

When the Exxon CEO Lee Raymond was asked by Congress why a merger with Mobil was necessary, each among the largest corporations in the world, he said, "We are not large enough. Economy of scale." And he said it with a straight face.

FOUR

Distinctions for the Common Good

Stimulating reflection rather than prescription gives
people the power to name the world. Prescription is
the key element between oppressed and oppressor.
Act of naming is the right of every person.

PAULO FREIRE

Before exploring how shifts in the fields of journalism, architecture, religion, and the neighborhood are essential to expanding the counternarrative of the common good, we want to detail the distinctions between the business perspective and the common good. This comparison is intended to make the choice clear and also to express the value in both belief systems.

1. Measures of Well-Being

Business Perspective: Capital, Income

Under the business perspective we regularly publish measures of the total monetary value of goods and services produced in the last quarter. We call this Gross Domestic Product. We measure average annual income by individuals and families. This is computed by dividing GDP by the population. We publicize the Dow Jones Industrial Average as a measure of well-being. We track consumer spending, new housing starts, high schools by rates of college admissions, children by grade point average and college entrance. Most of our measures declare that dollars produced or spent or earned define who we are and how we are doing.

Common Good Perspective: Well-Being, Trust

Under the common good we publish the measures of what economist Mark Anielski calls "genuine well-being." These measures are about the levels of trust people feel in those around them, the satisfaction and sense of security people feel where they live, the level of help and support people receive from neighbors, the trust and confidence people feel toward local governance and leadership, and whether people feel secure in the amount of money they have to lead a life they desire. We measure the local circulation of money. We measure education by children knowing what they are good at and their optimism about their own future.

2. Cost and Scale

Business Perspective: Global, Large, Online

We seek products with the lowest cost and most convenience, regardless of where they are produced. We produce goods and services most amenable to scale and widest distribution. We shop at the mall and big-box stores, and we prefer chain stores and franchises for their convenience, wide selection, ease of parking, food service, and prices. We shop online. We consider ourselves global citizens. The number of likes to our social media posts are an indication of our value and standing in the eyes of others. We prefer text over e-mail over phone calls. We celebrate anything that goes viral and imbue it with a sense of magic. We measure our work and business by their revenue growth and, in general, treat volume and size and the number of people who come to events as primary measures of impact. We measure social impact by level of funding or how many attend Sunday services.

Common Good Perspective: Local, Small, within Reach

Primary time, energy, and attention go to local relationships and patronage, supporting neighborhood places. We favor local farmers' markets, things locally produced, independent businesses. We prefer face-to-face meetings. Social life is organized into small events and encounters. We participate in associational life: book clubs, church groups, garden clubs, nature centers, library events, regular gatherings in coffee shops. Our focus is on local politics and on community issues concerning land and education and safety. We like online services for the information they offer, but don't believe they constitute civic engagement.

3. Competition and Cooperation

Business Perspective: Competitive, Individualistic

The business perspective values competitiveness and views it as the primary nature of a human being. It interprets Darwin's research as the survival of the fittest and considers grade competition to be useful for learning and for the way it helps in the sorting and selection process. Compensation is based on comparing peers at work. Individual accomplishment is the prime measure of value and usefulness. Upward mobility is considered the point of work, a key to motivating people and the proof of good parenting. In the church the individual's personal relationship with God is the central point. Outside the church we are wary of strangers and believe that if people are marginalized, economically isolated, or of low spirits, it is their responsibility, and we help them in the form of charity, human services, and goodwill. When we speak about our children, it begins with their job title or SAT scores. In the business perspective, people who have concerns with all of this are considered outliers and dreamers.

Common Good Perspective: Cooperative, Collective

The common good perspective views cooperation as the primary nature of human beings. We interpret Darwin's research as survival of the most cooperative. Organizational success is seen to be a result of team effort, and we design compensation and work structures to reflect that. The good life is defined as the level of engagement in the community and the quality of people's relationships. Church is a gathering place for bringing compassion, forgiveness, and God's message into the world outside the boundaries of the institution. We value stability and caring for a place and a community over a long period of time. In small towns we seek to keep the next generation at home and productive. We believe that all learning is social, meaning that learners learn best from each other. We know that care for the planet is in all of our hands. We consider people committed to the common good to be neighbors regardless of differing points of view.

4. Pace and Control

Business Perspective: Speed, Consistency, Predictability

The business perspective dislikes surprise and sees it as a weakness in planning and management. The primary question is whether what we are doing is replicable. We measure performance by consistency and seek to minimize human involvement for the sake of speed and accuracy. We love the autobahn for its lack of speed limits. In the consumer world humans in the customer service process are considered "friction." They cost time and money. The key question is, how long will something take? Service in all domains is measured by waiting time. The purpose of the interstate highway system is to produce economic growth. We love Siri, Alexa, and voice commands for phone calls and operating in an automated world. Fast food was not accidentally named.

Common Good Perspective: Depth, Slow, Surprise

The common good perspective values depth over speed. We are part of the slow food and slow money movements. We *like* surprise and believe it signals innovation and creativity. Craft and handmade are icons of the common good. We turn streets into pedestrian malls and create walkways, hiking trails, and bicycle lanes. Dissenters are welcome to stay in the circle. Strangers are welcomed and seen as a source of newness and vitality. We want a walkable city and life. On most nights we actually sit down to a dinner that was home-cooked.

5. Role of the Person

Business Perspective: Consumer, Commodity

Under the business perspective the primary interest in the person is as a consumer and as cost-effective, efficient labor. Ownership and control are centralized within a few hands. The simpler the task can be designed, the better to manage and leverage. People are considered replaceable commodities. In the business narrative we are eternally puzzled when people want to work at home and don't want to go back to the office, to trucking, or to service jobs they held before. We "acquire" talent when we hire. We believe that people's choices and behavior are primarily motivated by money and self-interest. That the sole role of the corporation is monetary return to stockholders. We believe that the more aspects of life that can be outsourced to experts and professionals, the better the outcomes and our well-being. We see health, children, safety, and care to be concerns that are enhanced by better services, management, and researched expertise. Public servants see people as customers.

Common Good Perspective: Producer, Unique Citizen

In the common good narrative the primary role of the person is as citizen. *Citizen* means people have the instinct and the cooperative capacity to produce, with others, their own well-being. Workplaces are cooperative ventures and can be communally owned and managed. Employees are motivated by purpose and peers—and they also are paid accordingly. People, including teenagers, can in every instance produce value. People with disabilities, with prison records, with low incomes, and those mistakenly called poor or homeless—all are people who have gifts and the capacity to offer them to all of us. We view putting labels on people to not be useful. We borrow from neighbors and have one forty-foot ladder and snow blower per fifteen households.

6. Context for Satisfaction

Business Perspective: Scarcity, More

The core belief of the business perspective is collective scarcity. Whatever the venue or concern, there is not enough. Not enough money, wealth, personal accomplishment, water, land, market dominance. Markets count on dissatisfaction. Our bodies are not strong, flexible, thin, tall, attractive, or famous enough. We are not loved enough, seen enough, appreciated enough. Whatever we have in terms of security, land, control, status, art, shoes, it is not enough. And if we do not have enough, then we are not enough. And this belief is in the nature of the world and our own existence. The playing field is essentially level. Success is up to you; all boots have straps.

Common Good Perspective: Abundance, Enough

The common good's core belief is collective abundance. Whatever the venue or domain, there is enough. If we can but see the situation or the condition more clearly and identify the available gifts, satisfaction and meaning can almost always be within reach. Even for those who do not participate in the dominant cultural narrative. On issues such as food, housing, well-being, there is enough. We just need to collectively focus on effective ways of shifting the distribution and exchange. This perspective is not about charity. Or providing more training or mentoring. Each person and group possesses the skills and capacities to have control over their own lives. This is the promise of the common good perspective: *ubuntu*. Same with the planet and the environment: We have the capacity to live within our means and do it by choice and being part of the earth. And we do it without waiting for someone else's transformation. We count on imagination more than proof or evidence.

7. Ownership

Business Perspective: Private

In the business narrative the assets of the world are best served by private ownership and control. *Our* ownership and control if we are a nation or an institution or organization. And we must maximize our gain for the present moment. This is the cornerstone of how we approach all that we deem to be valuable. Land. Markets. Language. Religion. Borders. This is the business case for the Doctrine of Discovery, Manifest Destiny, colonialism, eminent domain, and the commercialization of the earth's resources. This includes public–private partnerships, which use public dollars for private investment. The good life is finding an island for sale and buying it. Having my own snow blower.

Common Good Perspective: Communal, Not Government

The essence of the common good is to preserve traditions, cultures, and the earth for future generations. It believes in communal control of the land and its use. This includes taking land off the market so that living here remains affordable. Conversations about sustainability include how we encourage neighborliness as well as the environment. Where there are state, province, national, or global efforts, we support and work to bring them to where we live. What the common good is waiting for is for us to imagine that this counterstory can become the dominant narrative for the future we want to create and sustain.

The Collective Transformation

The challenge we face is that we have insufficient language and research about our collective and communal nature. Even though it is likely more amenable to change than individual tendencies. We have made progress in individual transformation, which is the enlightened side of individualism. Mindfulness, yoga, meditation. But it is still individualism. It does not translate well to the collective. It never mentions the land, and our safety, and making a living within walking distance. It takes advantage of groups, like eastern Sadhanas, therapy groups, AA and Al-Anon meetings. Bringing about collective transformation through peer connection rather than individual development or better leaders is what needs to be more common and more widely understood.

Our focus on the individual too easily mistakes liberation, which is the absence of oppression, for freedom, the capacity to create a world of our choosing. We underplay the importance of community connection for full expression of the self. Focusing on the communal possibility is the alternative to conversations about excess. About the problems with the centralization of capital, corporate dominance, monopolies, and the racist banking system. And with the ruling and elite classes.

The conversation, research, programs about these problems do not open the possibility of an alternative future. Too often our conventional view of the world and one another remains distorted. In Raj Patel's words: "The 'free market' belief is that we can, through the unrestricted exercise of supply and demand, make the world more perfect. This is not only delusional—it also distorts the way we see other people. Seeing fellow human beings as mere co-consumers blinds us to the deeper connections between us, and distorts our political choices."[15]

Gifts May Be the Point

Community and the common good are best defined by focusing on gifts in a culture that is currently organized around deficiencies. A vernacular or subsistence culture is based on what people can do now. It organizes citizens to create for themselves the human well-being that the modern world thinks must be purchased. Before the postwar surge of consumerism and development since the 1940s, subsistence living was honored. "Being a peasant" was a phrase implying respect and self-sufficiency.

With its ethos of gifts and self-sufficiency, community living gives rise to an economy of compassion. It affirms a theology based on fallibility, covenant, and mystery. This ethos supports journalism that is generative. It nurtures the prophetic quality of art and supports architecture that is welcoming and evokes aliveness. It also shifts our thinking about what measures matter. The common good perspective would have us measure trust, connectedness, efforts to make a place better—core elements of social capital. This creates a different narrative about who we are and what matters.

What would the shift to the common good narrative require? We would translate the Exodus story into today's terms, which calls us to depart the business perspective and its delivery system, the consumer culture. It calls for a relational activism based on several core ideas:

- **We make visible and important the work of citizens exercising the capacity to produce their own well-being.** We thrive in the modern wilderness and live into the belief that what we care most about cannot be purchased, professionally programmed, serviced, or incentivized. This counterstory develops a discipline of community that teaches and defines vital elements of how to grow social capital: building trust and making a place better together.

- **We end economic and neighborly isolation with leadership that supports activism based on the methodologies of lateral and peer relatedness.** How we engage people when we gather is decisive. Relational activism is organizing citizens to first connect with each other, then pursue together what they care most about. In this process we are indifferent to the labels we have traditionally used. The required transformations in leadership and activism are based in this counternarrative.

- **We focus the varied interests of activist movements as one movement.** That movement is citizen at the center. Our commitment to economic and racial justice, the planet, women's and indigenous rights, ending the system of prison bail and fines, and community-supported agriculture are pursued laterally, horizontally, among citizens and neighbors. They are all connected and the same thing. When this occurs, the politicians, executives, the people that look to be at the "top" will follow. Or not. We take our attention away from them. Let go of treating them as essential or making their support important. We thank them for taking on the burden of their role but don't make them the center of our attention.

The following chapters translate this discussion of our thinking, our narrative, our context into where concrete examples are now occurring. We give special focus to certain fields—local economies, journalism, religion, architecture, and the neighborhood—because they shape the way we experience our everyday lives and how we decide what matters and how to obtain it. These fields work on us in seen and unseen ways and thus can encourage us to adopt the common good perspective as we pursue improvement in the movements we are passionate about.

The reimagination in each of these fields is already under way. We only need to make it visible. And find ways to interweave what is occurring in all of them. No field on its own can undergo a transformation without joining and engaging the others. Journalism controls the story of it all. Architecture impacts the structure of a neighborhood. Religion holds the language of possibility, creates a context for journalism, and is a presence in almost every neighborhood. Together, all are needed to create an alternative future.

We don't see things as they are. We see things as we are.

ANAÏS NIN

FIVE

A Just Economy

I bought a wastepaper basket and carried it
home in a paper bag. And when I got home, I put
the paper bag in the wastepaper basket.

LILY TOMLIN

One of the core intentions of the common good is to support an economy that aligns with our other interests. The common good movement often focuses on the importance of our economy. It might be useful to expand what a shift in economic practice would entail. The intention is that this will give us more choice over how we relate to the market.

A Counternarrative Specific:
Ending Our Idea of Poverty

Poverty, as we know it, is the most common word we use to label economically vulnerable people. Even though we feed more people and declare low incomes are rising, much of human suffering in the form of *poverty* has been immune to treatment. We have declared war on poverty. We research and measure it. We have a large social-service industry of programs, job training, free schooling, diversity efforts, all of which *care* for the suffering and economically isolated and are worth doing. We talk of lifting people out of poverty, but it is us doing the "lifting" and leaving poverty behind. Underlying all of this is a modern lack of respect expressed when we call people "poor." In this label, and in the charity we send their way, we declare them broken.

This is our inherited view of poverty and the poor. A different view is that what we call poverty is more about their isolation than it is about their annual income. The stories we tell ourselves about why people are poor influence our view of them as well as our response. The director of the Othering and Belonging Institute, john a. powell, understands that calling someone "poor" is a case of mistaken identity. He writes: "In a wealthy and mature democracy, poverty is largely about social exclusion and the lack of belonging, not material inequality....Although some categories of persons are almost always considered 'deserving' of our support—children, for example—others are not....The stories we understand or tell ourselves about why people are poor matter."[16]

Shifting the Story

If transformation begins with a shift in narrative, then the way we think or speak of people we call poor is what needs to shift. Poverty can only be impacted by beginning to shift the story or construct we have about it.

- Rather than use the term *poor*, *poverty* is better named and conceived as a condition of economic isolation. Something shifts when we stop using the term *poverty*. Relational activism acts to end the isolation of the people we are concerned about. Economic isolation is a communal distress. It is a neighborhood condition. It is not the aggregation of individual deficiencies or a generational inevitability. Your future is not dictated by the zip code of your birth. It may be historically true, and useful to gain attention, but it is not decisive or useful.

- Building community and activating the common good creates the only condition where economic isolation can be converted. This occurs by focusing on people's gifts and productive capacities. Our work is to support projects that treat isolation, land ownership, stable housing, and local livelihood as communal endeavors. These efforts recognize that every neighborhood has a local culture, often a proud memory, and people taking care of each other. There is no place rightly labeled as an underserved neighborhood.

- Shifting the story would mean that in the philanthropy and social-service domains we stop funding services aimed at treating deficiencies and instead fund work that builds social capital and discovers what people in neighborhoods of interest are good at. The Financial Independence Initiative rewards people for tracking their own spending patterns. Starfire Council in Cincinnati rewards families with people with disabilities for joining with neighbors on local projects.

- Reclaiming and restoring the commons stops labeling people by their needs. We agree there is no such thing as a "poor" person. A "homeless" person. A "disabled" person. A high school "dropout." An "ex-offender." By shifting the language, we recognize and enhance conditions where trust and relatedness can occur. Where neighbors' relationship with each other becomes the focus. Where the gifts of these residents are vital to who they are. Where we call people simply by their names. There are places where this is occurring, which we discuss as we work through the fields of interest.

We can depart the consumer culture by declaring we are not primarily consumers and we are not constantly dissatisfied. Reclaiming control of our well-being comes from citizens not outsourcing what we can produce ourselves: able children, welcoming streets, a strong and beloved planet, health, social equity, and belonging. The consumer culture cannot sustain its power when we decide we are capable citizens who can accept the life we are living. That what *we* have is enough. That *I* am enough.

Moving to a future distinct from the consumer culture begins with small groups (friends, neighbors) and larger groups (faith groups, other values-driven organizations) who share an interest in our common concerns. This is no easy task, especially in the domain of land and development.

Our Land

Reverend Damon Lynch III, pastor of New Prospect Baptist Church in Cincinnati, Ohio, has engaged his ministry into the center of the conversation on racial justice. He understands that racial reconciliation has to do with control of the land. Displacement occurs when low-income people are moved out of a neighborhood to make room for new, market-driven construction. This is a contemporary version of the plantation. Damon often refers to the Kenyon Barr neighborhood of Cincinnati, where in 1960 twenty-six hundred buildings were torn down to build an industrial park and twenty-six thousand Black residents were displaced. The taking of land in the past is painful, Damon declares, but the taking of land in the present, within walking distance, is even more painful.

The reverend reminds us that after the Civil War, reparations took the form of offering land. We have a long history of taking the land, and only one brief moment of returning it. His version:

> In 1865, William T. Sherman signed something called Special Order 15. Special Order 15 was after slavery ended and gave 400,000 acres of tillable land to freed slaves because there was an understanding at that point in America, that after 246 years of slavery, America owed these people. Special Order 15 was signed into law. Three of its parts are relevant here:

> Section One: "The islands from Charleston, south, the abandoned rice fields along the rivers for 30 miles back from the sea, and the country bordering the St. Johns River, Florida, are reserved and set apart for the settlement of Negroes now made free by the acts of war and the proclamation of the President of the United States."

> Section Two specifies that these new communities would be governed entirely by black people themselves: "On the

islands, and in the settlements hereafter to be established, no white person whatever, unless military officers and soldiers detailed for duty, will be permitted to reside; and the sole and exclusive management of affairs will be left to the free people themselves."

Finally, Section Three specifies the allocation of land: "Each family shall have a plot of not more than 40 acres of tillable ground. When it borders on some water channel and not more than 800 feet waterfront, in the possession of which land the military authorities will afford them protection."

What became of the land that was promised? Abraham Lincoln, one day, goes to watch a play and he's sitting in the balcony. John Wilkes Booth walks up behind him and puts a bullet into his head. Andrew Johnson comes into the White House and immediately rescinds Special Order 15. Andrew Johnson has the land confiscated.

The final Union soldiers left the land in 1877.[17]

Displacement

Gentrification is a term for development that has spread throughout Black and minority communities in America. It is also called *displacement*. Its effect is to destabilize minority neighborhoods. This is done by calling them dangerous, underserved slums, beyond repair. It is accomplished by moving businesses and families out to serve the majority business interests. Various government efforts to remedy economic and housing discrimination have failed, in part because they succumb to the business perspective. One such effort is the Community Reinvestment Act (CRA), passed in 1977, requiring banks to compensate for decades of redlining, which meant few mortgages for Black people and majority-Black neighborhoods. Although banks are required by law to loan a percentage of mortgages to low-income neighborhoods, it turns out that they only have to issue loans in those zip codes. Most of those loans go to construct large buildings for health-care systems and universities. Very few of the mortgages go to increase Black homeownership or enterprise. This practice follows the letter but not the spirit of the law, and one local bank was fined $100 million for subverting the intent of the CRA.

Another form of supposed reparation is Opportunity Zones, which offer tax relief for investments in "economically disadvantaged" neighborhoods. This program has mostly turned these poor communities into tax shelters for the wealthy, ignoring the real economic and housing needs of the economically isolated residents. Among the many organizations interested in such developments is the Democracy Collaborative (TDC), a research and development organization focused on community wealth building. Founded in 2000, the Democracy Collaborative seeks out strategies that enhance community revitalization through inclusive and democratic ownership models.

In the mid-2000s the Democracy Collaborative coined the term *community wealth building* to describe efforts emerging around the country to advance a form of economic development based on democratic forms of ownership and control. As Nishani Frazier explained: "The building block of economic and social stability is work, home, and community....Two revitalization phenomena in particular—gentrification and opportunity zones—expressly imperil community development efforts across the United States....Recent evidence has already suggested that opportunity zones have increased sale prices for property owners compared to eligible tracts that weren't selected."[18]

The Development Myth

In his book on modernism, *When All That Is Solid Melts into Air,* Marshall Berman uses Goethe's Faust as an icon of the modern era and its affection for development. Faust becomes what we call a "developer." Paraphrasing Berman:

> Faust outlines a great reclamation project to create new towns and cities out of a barren wasteland. Goethe's Faust is an archetypal modern hero who strives to create a world where personal growth and social progress can be had without significant human costs.

> As Faust surveys his work, only a small piece of ground along the coast remains occupied by a sweet old couple, Philemon and Baucis. Even though Faust offers them a cash settlement or resettlement on a new estate, they refuse to move.

> At this point, he summons Mephisto (Satan) and his "mighty men" and orders them to get the old people out of the way. He does not want to see it or know the details of how it is done. He wants to see the land cleared next morning, so the new construction can start.

Mephisto and his special unit return in "deep night" with the good news that all has been taken care of. Faust, suddenly concerned, asks where the old folks have been moved—and learns their house has been burned to the ground and they have been killed. Faust is aghast and enraged. He protests that he didn't say anything about violence. Faust has been pretending not only to others but to himself that he could create a new world with clean hands. First he contracted out all the dirty work of development; now he washes his hands of the job, and disavows the jobber once the work is done.[19]

This is another window into the complexity of the business perspective. The promise of development is so compelling. The relational and communal price of "progress" is so hard to grasp. The modern skyscraper and new stadium are so visible. The expanse and allure of the suburb so clear. In addition to the attraction of land development, development calls to us in many ways. The reach of the Internet and iPhone, which can immediately answer every question and ease every purchase, isolates us and our children as surely as gentrification and displacement.

The Casualties of Culture, Community, and Place

The societal cost to seeking modernist versions of development is that we lose our cultural memory, our communal traditions, and our affection for "place." This results in abandoning our natural instinct to care for common interests. It takes a toll on our humanity. And our faith. We abandon our idealism in the name of "reality." Reality TV is the narrative of our least human selves. In fact, what we call reality on TV is almost totally scripted. Scripted reality. Virtual reality. It is time for a dating service for avatars.

As previously mentioned, "development," in addition to land, includes attempts to reform all aspects of our lives with technology, streamlining, and controls. All these efforts can be considered the protocols of empire—"royal protocols," according to Walter Brueggemann. The word *protocol* is useful because it clarifies that what is occurring is not on the shoulders of particular leaders, but on a set of practices and structures larger than any individual and produced with all of our participation. That is why changing leaders changes little. We want someone to blame, like Faust. We blame top management, or the current administration, but it makes little difference. It just feels good at the moment. Like any addiction.

One long-advocated program for economic justice is a guaranteed annual income. This proposed program is discussed by Ed Whitfield, cofounder and co-managing director of the Fund for Democratic Communities. In the article "We Don't Need Butter, We Need the Cow," Whitfield states his concern about a universal guaranteed annual income. A guaranteed income is basically "more widely available welfare." He says: "Our economy suffers from the fact that communities are not having their needs met and a quality of life equitably elevated by all. Neither the self-regulated market nor the intervention of government has been successful in doing this to the satisfaction of the many."[20]

Whitfield continues:

I'm reminded of a story....

A Black South African, Tabo, confronted a White man, Mr. Smith, who had disrespected him and stolen his prize cow. With the prospect of amnesty for telling the truth, the White man admitted to having done what he was accused of, recognized how horribly wrong it was, and asked for forgiveness, saying that he was truly sorry. Tabo was visibly relieved for having an opportunity to confront his oppressor and get an apology. They shook hands and embraced. As Mr. Smith stood to leave, free, with his amnesty, the Black man called out to stop him. The White man turned back with a questioning look on his face, not sure why he was being stopped. Tabo, the Black South African, asked him, "But what about the cow?" Mr. Smith was visibly angry: "You are ruining our reconciliation," he shouted, "This has nothing to do with a cow." That is the question we must ask all those who say the past is long gone but still retain ownership of the herd produced by that old cow. We won't forgive and forget until we get the cow back....Suppose that the Mr. Smiths in the world make a counteroffer: "I'll tell you what, why don't I just give you a supply of butter?" "The hell," Tabo might reply. "If you give me back my cow, I can give you butter!..."

What I do think we need is reparations, the democratization of wealth, the re-creation of the commons, and the outlawing of financial systems of theft and speculation. Communities must become their own developers through broadly democratic planning and democratic access to non-extractive financing....

The key is democracy and expanded opportunities to be
productive rather than consumption. We need the cow back,
not just a supply of butter.[21]

Jubilee and a Just Economy

Adam Clark, professor of theology at Xavier University, talks about
economic justice for the Black community and the idea of Jubilee
as part of a counternarrative. Biblical jubilee means forgiving debts
every seven years, restoring the land to the citizens every forty-nine
years. As Clark explains:

> To really think of a vision to unite us in ways that are healthy
> and holistic is a very challenging counter-cultural thing to do.
> That's where the word "jubilee" comes in. Jubilee is a biblical
> metaphor…a period of economic re-distribution where slaves
> are set free, land is returned to its original owners and debts are
> forgiven.
>
> How do we think about jubilee, in light of consumerism—our
> new religion. It's probably the most dominant religion in the
> world. Because it's not just production and exchange. We're
> talking about how human beings produce meaning for their
> lives.
>
> Our practices of consumption are related to what some refer
> to as the politics of disposability. For us to maintain this certain
> level of wealth and power in our side of the world, we have to
> make people on the other side of the world, or on the other side
> of our community, disposable.[22]

The market is a problem in its current form as it defines our way of living and our social relations. As this book's opening epigraph by Robert Inchausti states, the executive has replaced the bishop, the king, and the professor as the source of wisdom and influence.

The cost is that as citizens we become commodified. Customers. Laborers. Labeled generations. Millennials. Gen X and Gen Z. We become objects instead of subjects. Our homes and extra bedrooms are now commercialized as bed and breakfasts, our cars become taxis, both romanticized as part of "the sharing economy." Each of us witnesses and participates in this world. There is no blame, for we have all created this market-minded world. The executives are simply delivering what we ask them to do. We can blame the wealthy, but that does not take us anywhere. They do not buy lottery tickets. We buy lottery tickets and sustain the growth of sports betting.

Summing Up

We create an opening for a new perspective when we see clearly the historical business narrative, name it, and accept it for what it is. It is a very popular story. It has its value. It is not, however, our nature, nor is it inevitable. This acceptance, seeing it without judgment, is difficult and necessary. We can work to change the workings of the narrative, but our primary work together is to create and give form to another context or perspective. The chapters that follow explore examples of where this other context exists now, sorted by the fields of interest where they occur.

The enemy of truth is not error. The enemy of truth is certainty.

BRUCE GREGORY

SIX

Religion beyond Boundaries

Fear knocked at the door,

Faith answered, and no one was there.

UNKNOWN

A key field of interest and opportunity for the common good is religion. Many contemporary congregations are rethinking how they can more powerfully act on their beliefs. Historically many Western religions have focused on bringing new people into the building and converting them into their form of worship. Or sending missionaries to other countries or adopting congregations in other neighborhoods.

This is increasingly being questioned in some faith communities. They are noticing that much of their good works have operated under the business perspective. Charity does not level the playing field; instead it holds that people who fail in the modern economy need our generosity. That they need programs to "lift them up," give them clothing, housing, and food. Build skills to compete in the free market. But some faith communities are no longer judging their impact by weekly attendance and the number of meals served in their programs. Some are even selling their buildings and becoming conveners in the neighborhood. They are social innovators bringing the language and sacred intention of the faith community beyond the property lines and into local economies and new physical spaces. They are being relational activists and creating new forms of the common good.

We Don't Need Evidence

Religion in this context does not exclusively have to do with a belief in God. Or a higher power. Or a spiritual journey. In its simplest terms, *religion* as used here is faith and its capacity to create room for uncertainty and what is unknowable and to bring this inquiry into the world. *Faith* is the willingness to create a future that is not based on evidence. If we had irrefutable evidence, we would not need faith. *Faith* is simply the choice to engage the world, run for office, plant an orchard, keep land off the market, hold services in a public place, or help neighbors produce their own marketplace. This is where religion and the common good intersect.

When we look at religion as a field of interest, the conversation becomes "What is our community up to, and how do we learn from that, join that, and initiate more?" This conversation replaces traditional concerns about growing the congregation. The business perspective too often dominates traditional religious practices. As hinted above, this includes charity, where we too often consider ourselves as healed and others as broken. And missionary work, in urban centers in the United States as well as in Africa and Latin America, where we believe *they* need what *we* have. Perhaps we can save them. Paint their buildings, teach them about health, improve their education. Charity is generous but does not produce equity.

Religious communities often hold tightly to their endowments and have trustees committed to protect them. This means they take a strict business approach in how they invest and what they fund. Consistency, control, and predictability become core criteria. But money and faith have a very awkward relationship. Some activists in the philanthropy industry are seeing how toxic and colonial it can be when exercising control in the midst of surplus.[23]

The Religion of the Market

Before we offer examples of the common good perspective already present in religion, David Loy, through his books and his essay "The Religion of the Market," shifts the context in which we think of religion. He expands our view to see how religion can be the means by which the rainforests can be restored and wealth disparity can be eliminated. Loy believes that a shift in economics is inseparable from a shift in religion. He talks of how the dominant narrative of scarcity economics is a compensation for an emptiness in faith. And how religion tries to fill that void.

In Loy's words:

> Today the most powerful alternative explanation of the world is science, and the most attractive value system has become consumerism. Their academic offspring is economics, probably the most influential of the "social sciences."[24]

> Our present economic system should also be understood as our religion, because it has come to fulfill a religious function for us. The discipline of economics is less a science than the

theology of that religion, and its god, the Market, has become a vicious circle of ever-increasing production and consumption by pretending to offer a secular salvation.[25]

The Common Good in Motion

My friend Father Joe Kovitch, an Episcopalian priest, says that the institution of religion has commodified faith and made it transactional. Religion can fall victim to a market mentality of them-and-us isolation—profit over prophet. The business perspective has influenced faith to lessen and control the impact of prophetic mercy and justice, thus preventing authentic partnerships and collaborations in the interest of the common good. What follows below are four examples of faith communities that have reimagined their work in the world. All in the direction of the common good: valuing the gifts of people regardless of income, being touched by the other, and committed to equity in all its forms.

More Than Programs

Choosing the common good is to let go of one's credentialed and traditional role in society. In this example it takes the form of a congregation shifting their thinking from offering church programming to practices that engage their members, neighbors, and strangers as coproducers of well-being. In the words of Pastor Mike Mather, it is "to name the gifts, talents, dreams, and passions of our neighbors, celebrate and bless those gifts, and connect them to other people who care about the same thing."[26]

Mike began his shift in thinking when leading Broadway Methodist

Church in Indianapolis, a large urban church trying to understand what it means to be a good neighbor in a diverse, economically isolated income area. After years of providing the traditional services to the neighborhood, Mike and his church realized that the neighborhood wasn't changing for the better. In his words:

> Across the years the congregation continued to think about what it meant to be in ministry in a low-income community. We started summer recreation programs, tutoring programs, and food pantries. Then nine young men under 25 years old died around here in just nine months. It caused us to ask whether in doing these good works, were we really changing things on the ground the way we had intended? It makes us, the congregation, feel good, but it doesn't really change things. We decided we just weren't going to do it anymore.[27]

Instead of running summer programs, they would hire young people from the community to become Roving Listeners. These listeners knocked on doors and asked about the gifts and talents of their neighbors and then connected them to each other.

> We have shifted our measures of the difference we make. What we pay attention to is does the economy get more stable, do dollars circulate more in people's hands, is there less violence, and are people happier?

> We also discovered when we began this work that things that we always thought were true weren't true. When we labeled the neighborhood as an unstable and low-income place, it affected

us in the ways in which we looked at the people. This does not define who they are.[28]

This is an example of the prophetic role the faith community can play. To end recreation and skill-building programs. To focus on the gifts of neighbors. To connect neighbors with complementary interests. To create livelihood by helping find a market for those skills and interests such as catering, child care, engine repair, and renovating buildings. More on this later in chapter ten on the neighborhood, where we hear from DeAmon Harges, the first Roving Listener.

A Place at the Table

When the late Edd Conboy took over orchestrating the Breaking Bread meals at Broad Street Ministry, a secular outreach providing food and clothing to individuals in the Center City district of Philadelphia, he wanted to counteract the constant messages about being deficient that receivers of service encounter every day, like having to stand in line for food or clothing. He realized that waiting is one of the most powerful reinforcers of the class system. It symbolizes helplessness, hopelessness, and the constant concern that there is not enough—and that it might run out just before it is my turn.

So Edd and the congregation did something about that. They took all the pews out of a large and prominent old church to make space for about two hundred people to sit at round tables with tablecloths and regular dinnerware and silverware. In Edd's words:

> We try to use as few disposable things as possible because we think that gives a message to folks that they're our guests and that they are not disposable as well.

We really want them to have a feeling of being included and being part of something that is vital and vibrant. So, we don't have a soup kitchen model. Our focus is on the dining room. The food is really not our central focus. Our central focus is on hospitality. We have a hospitality model and think that radical hospitality leads to radical change.[29]

Volunteers serve their guests tableside; there is no standing in line for a meal, cafeteria style.

Another important piece of Broad Street's radical hospitality is encouraging volunteers to sit down and chat with their guests to get to know people living such a different life. As Edd explains:

Our sense is that many of our guests are experiencing housing insecurity or food insecurity, and are often living on the streets.

We have a sense that they have essentially forgotten who they are. We want to have a place and engagement where they can remember who they are and see that they are vital members of our society and culture. We want them to know that they matter and that we care about them and that we notice them.[30]

Edd's staff and volunteers address the chronic problem of scarcity in all of its forms. Their guests can sit anywhere they want, anytime they want. The volunteers learn from their guests how to engage with them in ways that are truly hospitable. The ministry uses a lottery system to allow small groups to access a clothes closet, where volunteers mend what guests already have and fit them with new clothes. Breaking Bread makes no spiritual demands on its guests and is in that sense secular, but the guests are aware of their surroundings.

Any one of these practices in a church can seem small. Yet small is where the future first occurs. Small puts the world in our own hands. Small can be profound, which is the case here. Relational activism takes forms like this, whether a way of making reservations for a meal, or a shift in what question we ask those in the room. When a new structure or question occurs, the change has occurred. Scale and funding are never the launching point in the common good perspective.

A Church Turned Inside Out

Father Joseph Kovitch, former priest of St. Matthew's Episcopal Community in Westerville, Ohio, led a congregation that sold their building and now sees the world as their parish. From meeting in an Irish pub on Sundays to purchasing a community house, the congregation has worked hard to identify who the community is and why the church exists. "It is not about painting the church by numbers," Father Joe says, "but growing our impact through deep hospitality, holy listening, and radical relationship."[31] Father Joe is not going out to get more people into a church building. His congregation is working to understand that the world is their parish.

Known as the village priest, Father Joe notes how faith communities are living into a future based on the common good narrative: "The thing that I see changing…is that we are tearing down our walls of separation to say, 'Can we join the conversation?' We have a church that needs to be evangelized by the greater community. They're amazingly spiritually gifted. The church is out there."[32] St. Matthew's is known for its community hospitality and takes pride in their Neighbor to Neighbor kindness groups. The process has broken silos and isolation. "We're not apologizing or giving up the core of Christ, the core of sacrament," Father Joe says, "but we're trying to live into the Sermon in the Mount. To live into the fact of radical hospitality and that we lead with love."[33]

A Radical Rabbi

Rabbi Miriam Terlinchamp leads Temple Sholom in Cincinnati, where her congregation chose their own way of shifting away from the business perspective toward the common good. After they developed a deeper appreciation of their connection to the community, Rabbi Miriam and the congregation began to view their large synagogue building and their finances in a new light. They decided to sell the building.

Then Rabbi Miriam radicalized the system that most synagogues use to raise money. Synagogue membership typically depends on honoring financial pledges. If someone doesn't pay their pledge, they are billed. If they don't pay the bill, they are dismissed from the congregation. Temple Shalom changed the way they handled the pledge debts owed to the synagogue. In keeping with this new spirit and as a way of "going first," Temple Sholom began to enact the Old Testament covenant of Jubilee, which is centered on the forgiveness of debt. All debt owed to Temple Sholom was forgiven. Members would decide the level at which they would fund the congregation. It extracted the rabbi from managing revenue generation and accounts receivable.

These two changes called for a new relationship with money—a relationship defined by a spirit of abundance rather than scarcity. "Debt cripples the soul," Rabbi Miriam says. "When you forgive a debt, you welcome someone in from exile. You are God's hands, ushering in a world of wholeness. Only when our relationships move from the transactional to the covenantal will we experience the genuine community we crave."[34]

Summing Up

These examples from the religious community find their counterparts in each of the other fields of interest that follow. They embody consciousness about the importance of reciprocal relationships, equity in all its forms, each finding its way to serve the common good.

A cult is a religion with no political power.

THOMAS WOLFE

SEVEN

Journalism of What Matters and What Works

When I was deputy press secretary at the White House our credibility was so bad we couldn't believe our own leaks.

BILL MOYERS

Journalism is the discipline that most explicitly voices the narrative of choice for a culture. At this moment that choice is the business perspective. Reimagining a journalism that supports the common good begins with what we think is worthy of our attention. One dimension of this questions whether change resides in the front office. The top floor. The oval office. The favorite centers of attention for the business perspective. If you believe in a culture of control, consistency, and predictability, then who is on top matters most.

The power of journalism is its capacity to define what constitutes news, whether reporting on commerce, politics, religion, public safety, entertainment, or social service. Counternarratives occurring in economics, religion, architecture, and neighborhoods have no real visibility without a journalism weaned away from the leaders and luminaries of the dominant culture. The following excerpt is from

Richard Cornuelle, a disquieting voice about who captures our attention. Read it as poetry rather than prescription:

"ENTER A PRIEST DISGUISED AS A PRIEST."

A stage instruction in an Elizabethan play

The superstition that America works because the front office manages it is reinforced every day by what we read in the papers. The American press is a front-office press. It reports America as if it were Oz, as if what is remarkable about society are the efforts to manage it. The more remote and authoritarian an institution, the more likely the press is to report its activities exhaustively. As a result, we are strangers to our own society....

The front office is desperately—sometimes exclusively— concerned with appearances, and with the perpetuation of the management illusion. The first question in the halls of authority is "How will it look?"—by which is meant "What will the reporters say about it?" Then the press dutifully reports as news what the front office has already decided would be news....

When I was at NAM (National Association of Manufacturers), everything we did, we did for the press. NAM existed exclusively for the press and was, in turn, a product of the press. NAM, a result of front-office mythology if there ever was one, was, in a sense, an illusion. It had no reality beyond the artificial news it created.

The press reports what is most readily reportable—beauty contests and prizefights and elections. Thus it has made the synthetic seem authentic and left the authentic unreported. You can put it down as a kind of law that the most important happenings have no spokespeople, no office of public relations, and hence no voice that is intelligible to the working press.[35]

The View from the Front Office

Here is a quote from the most prominent front office of all, the White House. It is from John Ehrlichman, assistant to President Richard M. Nixon, about the Nixon era. It is a telling example of what Cornuelle speaks of, using information fed to the media not to report but to manipulate. Ehrlichman said:

> You understand what I'm saying? We knew we couldn't make it illegal to be either against the war or blacks, but by getting the public to associate the hippies with marijuana and blacks with heroin, and then criminalizing both heavily, we could disrupt those communities. We could arrest their leaders. Raid their homes, break up their meetings, and vilify them night after night on the evening news. Did we know we were lying about the drugs? Of course we did.[36]

The narrative produced by our journalism is not a problem in the quality of its reporting or its passion for accuracy and investigation. It is built to tell the story: who, what, when, where, and why. It is based on its best effort at neutrality or not, elusive as that might be. And it is investigative. Seeking what is unseen, illegal, or in conflict. And what is tragic. And compelling and entertaining.

The question for journalism, and the business versus common good perspective, is what journalism considers news. The central element is about story selection. Most news reporting encourages the business perspective. One form of this is love of the miraculous promise of digital technology and science. This includes its risks. Every new chip and nuance of scale and convenience is fully reported. It markets the promise of technology and science to deliver magic. It believes that putting a cell phone in the hands of the marginalized will reduce poverty. That more discovery of the cellular components of our brain and pinpointing where our capacity to love resides will make us more loving. It believes that more digital disruption of businesses will elevate our lives. And that science will end global warming, if there is such a thing.

Journalism also has a deep fascination for what leaders do. What are politicians and very rich people tweeting? These are heavily reported. What policies are being debated and who disagrees? What is missing in this is considering that what is working among citizens is vital headline news. What is needed is journalism committed to the common good. It would embody several qualities:

- First, it would not feed on what is sensational and bolsters the attention economy. It would choose depth and uniqueness. Let the common good in normal doses be important. Let's not celebrate scale or what goes viral.

- Journalism runs on the headline. Above the fold. The banner across the flat screen. Instead of bleeding and leading, report on what is innovative and working in the lives of citizens. Put aside the affection for the suffering and violence that is always

available. We live in the strange condition where crime is going
down and the reporting and fear of crime are going up.[37]

- Report on where agreement exists in the world. Covering both
  sides of a story is not served by reporting on the extremes.
  Agreement can be as interesting and surprising as conflict.
  Like the question of where opposites are attracting one
  another for a larger purpose.

Common Good Journalism

There have been several efforts to move in the direction of journalism committed to the common good. One example is civic journalism, a concept that allows reporters to use their standing and skills
to improve civic life.

Common good journalism is simply curious and frames things ap-
preciatively. It focuses on the gifts and capacities of our local efforts
to build a society that works. It carries the storyline of how citizens
are creating their own well-being, the good and the struggle of it. It is
about where people are accountable for what they care about. About
where the climate is being locally cared for and not. It is about citizens who are struggling to produce their own safety, finding ways
for teenagers to be useful, all of us caring for the isolated, engaged in
local livelihood, attending to the beauty of nature, and struggling to
collectively own developed and undeveloped land. It is also concerned
with how the public can be involved in story sourcing, development,
and distribution in a way that sparks community engagement.

This requires reimagining who are the news makers. Broadening the perspective beyond those with power, money, and name recognition. It creates a counterstory to the dominant belief that all that matters occurs in big buildings and in the actions of the leaders, elected officials, presidents, and board members. People making policy, legislating, and campaigning are newsworthy, but not the headline. Policy matters, but common good journalism is most important when it follows what citizens are creating. If we choose to report on depth and meaning and the variability of culture, and philosophy, then we are expressing and touching real life. Reporting on how we are polarized is a simple, low-cost way to compete for attention.

Journalism grounded in the common good understands that residents, local activists, and social innovators on a human scale are creating a different community narrative. They are creating the future in an infinite number of ways, mostly unreported. This is why books such as David Bollier's *Commoner's Catalog for Changemaking* and Jay Walljasper's *All That We Share: How to Save the Economy, the Environment, the Internet, Democracy, Our Communities and Everything Else That Belongs to All of Us* are so important.

The news prides itself as being a cornerstone of protecting democracy. Of being the Fourth Estate. This will be honored the moment we understand that the neighborhood is where democracy is most alive. Where faith communities are most at work. Where the future is being created right now. Where architecture has its greatest impact. Maybe the catchphrase should be "if it heals, it leads." The common good is mostly immune to heroics, except for the strength it takes to persist in ordinary matters. Let us begin to treat people in charge and wrongdoers as human-interest stories. Put them in section three, near the end.

Also, journalism committed to the common good understands that the world is complicated, paradoxical. That there is a place for mystery and what is perhaps unknowable. That predictability is not all that is worth attention. Social intelligence and innovation stop taking a back seat to artificial intelligence. Common good reporting will cover where the shift is occurring in how we name the economically isolated and other labeled people. Below is an example of a headline story of where the common good is at work now.

Citizens and Police Producing Safety

Mike Butler for twenty-seven years was chief of public safety in Longmont, Colorado. He is a leading practitioner and voice for the common good. He brought the concept of restorative justice into the central strategy of public safety. Working with the criminal justice system, typically a top-down organization, Mike promoted a partnership orientation, giving a broad category of people a larger voice. His police department strongly supported restorative justice, which operates on the principles of repairing the harm done to victims of crime, with the offender choosing accountability and making amends, and the victim, their family, and the community considering forgiveness. This is an example of news that belongs on the front page and above the fold. In Mike's words:

> We still live in a society in which justice is defined as an eye
> for an eye or a pound of flesh; when you hear people say I
> want justice, that's what they are saying. In Longmont we
> have been able to make great strides in terms of changing the

> definition of what true justice can be. When we have sustained
> accountability it greatly reduces repeat offenders, when we
> have victims walking away saying I feel much more whole....
> You, as the Police Department, are the convening agent. An
> invitation to a conversation other than what the police are
> going to do to keep you safe and punish the offender.[38]

The conversation here is among the offender and their family, the victim and their family, and members of the community. It has four elements: admission of guilt, apology for the crime, a commitment to not do it again, and an agreement to provide restitution to the victim or community. The victim and community have to decide whether to believe the offender. If they do not, the offender reverts to the judicial system. These conversations occur under the auspices of the police department.

Thousands of offenders in Longmont have become useful citizens coming out of the restorative process and avoiding the complex impacts of entering the court and prison system. Thousands of citizens have offered their time and consideration to finding ways to help offenders reclaim their lives. There is more to the story of how Longmont citizens have brought their gifts and generosity to people economically and socially isolated in their community, at times even inviting strangers into their homes. All initiated by the police chief and his team working as conveners and hosts to citizens willing to take part in the well-being of their city. And doing it slowly, over a period of time, and as part of the normal way of operating. This is transformation. This is relational activism called forth by a traditional institution. This is news.

News Focusing on Local Actions

The common good is human, local, and textured. Common good journalism is willing to write about events that are local and complicated. Here are some news organizations that are focused on local actions and struggles, where regular citizens, for better or sometimes not, are pursuing our collective and authentic well-being:

Yes! **magazine**. For a long while, *Yes!* has reported on the issues of economics, housing, climate, governance, services, and the power of so-called marginalized people. Their reporting is mostly about what is working and about what local people are accomplishing around the world. They publish articles about where local action is worthy of being called news.

Milwaukee Neighborhood News Service. Housed in Marquette University, this news service publishes stories about what impacts neighborhood well-being. They report on neighborhood events and accomplishments and also on how art builds community. And their contributors are artists, writers, and musicians on a citizen scale. Like most new journalism news organizations, these efforts are mostly funded by a mix of subscriptions and donations.

Next City. Based in Detroit, this operation is committed to the neighborhood. It reports on the concerns of people at all levels and has a special interest in questions of equity and justice. It works to understand in depth what is at stake and what can be identified as possibilities for citizen cooperation. It is mostly online reporting, and at the end of the year it publishes, in print, the major success stories of people serving the common good. Next City journalism leads the way to performing a narrative that converts consumer to citizen and reconstructs what matters in our lives and our communities. In this way it is supremely political. In the words of Oscar Perry Abello, senior economic justice correspondent:

> You know the kind of journalism that sells the easiest. The click-bait kind, the gossip kind that's so much about how people abuse their power.
>
> We don't do that kind of work at Next City. We don't look down on it necessarily. Reporting on abuses of power is important to a functioning democracy, but the kind of journalism Next City produces reflects the belief that journalism must also report on those who are tapping into power that is less conspicuous and using it to change how things work around them in cities.[39]

There are many other news organizations doing similar work. A few more examples of common good journalism include:

Solutions Journalism Network. This network is influential in spreading an orientation of being a catalyst toward making things better and being constructive. Check out the story tracker on their website.

City Bureau. Located in Chicago, it has an initiative called Documenters, which was given money to spread their work to other cities. They train locals to cover public meetings. And pay them for doing it.

Axiom News Media Collaborative. Axiom News in Canada, led by Peter Pula, has made a profound commitment to cultivating community and acting as a powerful convener for the common good. They are currently hosting more than three hundred community gatherings and just getting started. Each gathering is focused on activating citizens to make their places better.

Dialogue journalism. Eve Pearlman and her team at Spaceship Media believe that connection and relationship are the starting place for good, useful journalism, and that awareness has always informed their reporting. They exemplify the work of a new breed of journalists who counter the notion that the work they produce is not informed by who they are. Eve says: "I knew each time I made a choice—what story to cover (or not), who to interview (or not), what data to include (or not), what questions to ask (or not), what quotes to use (or not)—those choices were informed by my definitions of importance and relevance, meaning and value, by who I was and where I came from."[40]

Dialogue journalism acknowledges that balanced reporting has become a cliché. Telling the story of both extremes does not constitute balance. It is participating in the marketing strategies of both sides. One project of Eve's was to interview people that represented a good cross section of the community and had divided points of view. This is another example of common good protocols and relational activism in the journalism setting. Her intention was to have a civic impact. They asked:

What do you want to know about the other side?

What do you want them to know about you?

What do you think about them?

What do you think they think about you?[41]

They then reported the responses back to the citizens. The impact helped produce civility. These questions build accountability and stop feeding alienation. They help people see that the other side is not so bad. One key was they, as journalists, were trusted because they showed up being honest about their own authentic selves, which is the essence of transformation.

Journalism transforming. In "New Ways to Tell the News," Paula Ellis, a news, corporate, and civic leader, currently a senior associate at the Kettering Foundation, talks about the changing nature of the news business and what's possible in emergent news models. She says: "The idea of objectivity was very dangerous and damaging to journalism. It was an economic idea, by the way. It wasn't a journalism idea. It was created as news organizations were monopolizing markets. We've created this master narrative that the world will be forever screwed up and cannot be fixed."[42]

What this means is that conventional news generates fear; the more fear, the easier it is to control citizens. It is the business perspective with a public face.

Journalism That Matters

In her "Open Letter to Journalists," Peggy Holman takes the reimagination of the journalist's job even further. She opens her letter: "It's time for a new compact between Journalists and the Public." Many people are negative about the press because they feel let down. Holman notes that if you don't feel trusted as a journalist, it is in part because the corporations you represent are not trusted. In these confusing times, journalism matters more than ever. Holman's letter spells out a new contract between reader and journalist.

Here is a sample of citizen requests:

- Treat me as a citizen first. As a consumer I don't need you. As a citizen, I do.

- Listen and engage with me in identifying and pursuing the stories that make a difference.

- Share with me your intention in telling a story, why you believe it matters for me to know. Stay with it even if I am slow to engage.

- Tell me stories through an appreciative eye, helping me to see not just the worst of the situation but the possibilities inherent in whatever is happening.

- Bring us together as a community. Engage us in conversations, helping us to hear one another's perspectives—even those that are different, uncomfortable—to uncover what matters to us all.

What the journalist offers:

- I'll tell you what I need, make you aware of the stories that matter to me.

- I'll offer you my story selection, my questions, as well as my information, knowledge, expertise, and creativity to support stories you care about.

- Together we'll get clear about what is newsworthy, what stories need to be told.

- When you speak to me of possibilities, I will engage, bringing my voice and energy to the issues that you raise.[43]

The common good needs a partnership between citizens and journalists, Holman says, because journalism is too important to leave just to professionals.

Summing Up

There are few people in a city that have relationships with a broader cross section of people than the journalist. They can connect to all sectors, leaders and citizens, rich and regular neighborhoods, all political leanings, giving them a perfect opportunity to host our community as well as describe it. The opportunity for journalism is that it is a field of interest that is visible and powerful. The challenge is that it is difficult to find funding and space in the attention world to create counternarrative stories, those for the common good. The reality is that consumers have always paid for the news. It is just taking a different form. Plus, the water has been muddied by considering social media as a news source. Social media has allowed high-profile people to circumvent the ethics and professionalism of traditional news outlets.

None of this diminishes the essential role of the news to celebrate and make visible the social innovations in the common good arena. This is a prime opportunity for citizens, who have the final choice of where we place our attention, to abstain from treating the news of fear, violence, and oppositional politics as if it matters. It might qualify as entertainment, but we can be witnesses to the drama without drawing conclusions from it about who we are and what is important to focus on and create together.

It is risky to be in a position of authority.

You have to watch the news to relax.

PETER KOESTENBAUM

EIGHT

Architecture of Aliveness

We shape our buildings,

and afterwards our buildings shape us.

WINSTON CHURCHILL

The interest of the commons is powerfully impacted by how we think of land and buildings. The physical space, interior and exterior, and our way of relating to the land carry either the story of the business perspective or honor the importance of how building and the land are foundational in bringing people into contact with each other and the earth. The business perspective is expressed by the suburbs replacing farmland, and the modernist love of efficiency, fondness for glass and steel, and worship of the front and corner office. The distinction can simply be seen in each built structure that can either be a testimony to the importance of economics and the architect or designed for the experience of the inhabitants and neighbors.

The business perspective narrative versus the common good narrative runs throughout the current and historical thinking about every acre of property. The dominant belief today, justified by philosopher John Locke many centuries ago, is that every piece of land should be viewed for its maximum economic value, including

so-called public land. This is the core practice of most urban planning programs, architecture schools, and the Urban Land Institute.
In the end an important part of the common good may be best served
by taking land off the market and away from speculation. The common good perspective can also view "undeveloped" land having value
in and of itself.

There is no place where the values of consistency and efficiency
are more visible than in the suburbs—Levittown, the first large sub-
urban development after World War II, being iconic. This development heralded the end of the front porch and its invitation to con-
viviality. Plus there is the garage door opener, which allows me to
enter my house without making eye contact, and the elimination of
sidewalks—all help us see how architecture impacts our ways of connecting and living with distance and privacy from those around us.

The interior design of our buildings also carries a statement of
how we choose to be together. It is about the intention of control versus engagement. To what extent does the interior design invite us
to build community, connect with each other, and embrace our collective interest? Consider how the open-space concept office, with
no walls, desks facing one direction and few windows, serves both
cost savings and ease-of-supervision agendas. Meeting rooms and
training spaces are dominated by large rectangular tables and often
arranged in U-shapes, with an open space in front for speakers and
their PowerPoints. Auditoriums and church sanctuaries with fixed
seating all facing the same direction also carry the message about
whose voice counts.

Architecture that supports the common good takes form in architect and design theorist Christopher Alexander's writing about
what structures have a quality of aliveness. This thinking leads us to

common land trusts and conservancies. Pocket neighborhoods and cohousing communities. Public gathering spaces. Schools, libraries, museums, and churches as community spaces. And make room for hip-hop architecture. Who would have thought?

The Alexander Quality of Aliveness

Christopher Alexander has influenced a generation of architects with the ideas in his books, two of which are *The Timeless Way of Building* and *A Pattern Language*. He writes about concepts for a pattern language that creates a quality of aliveness: "The specific patterns out of which a building or a town is made may be alive or dead. To the extent they are alive, they...set us free; but when they are dead, they keep us locked in inner conflict."[44]

Alexander's approach to this pattern language is a set of ground rules producing a sense of wholeness composed of interconnected centers or parts. Aliveness and wholeness can only happen through an "unfolding" process. Transformation unfolds as we become aware of the importance of each small step we take toward the whole. For example, if you design an outside balcony, it needs to be at least six feet wide. A room needs to have two entrances and windows in two walls. It needs window frames with splayed edges, windows that open wide, with small panes, letting in filtered light. This aliveness, Alexander says, is made up of separate centers where each center has a certain life or intensity. A center can be the planning process itself, each room in a house, a house in a neighborhood, a neighborhood in a city.

Alexander speaks from the world of architecture, and his focus is on buildings and towns. The reason he is especially important in our conversation is that his thinking about bringing that quality of aliveness into all that we do applies equally well to the creation of the common good. For this architect, *aliveness* is achieved by developing a pattern language. Our adaptation of this term is to create a narrative for the common good that strives for a sense of wholeness and a collection of centers for creating our collective well-being. In the absence of aliveness, we unknowingly experience an inner conflict, a feeling of something unresolved. This is one impact of the business perspective that counts on a culture where we are permanently unresolved, never enough and always needing more.

As with Alexander's discussion of aliveness and wholeness, in the evolution of the common good, an unfolding strategy requires giving an uncomfortable importance to each small step we take. In being guided by the narrative of the common good, we have to worry as much about the arrangement of a meeting room as we do about the issue on schools or racial justice that caused us to assemble. We must attend to the unfolding of a strategy, a program, an invitation, the questions for a gathering, or building a master plan. This approach leads us to value the details of each step so that it becomes its own center. Each step of a master plan has to be a small example of the qualities that we want in the final large thing.

Architecture and Social Impact

In *Keeping Faith: Philosophy and Race in America*, Cornel West, an American philosopher, political activist, and social critic, validates architecture as an important element of the commons by drawing a connection between power and authority and architecture. West writes:

> Architecture...is the last discipline in the humanities to be affected by the crisis of the professional and managerial elitism in American society....The political legitimacy of architecture is not a question of whether and why buildings should be made. Rather, it has to do with how authority warrants or does not warrant the way in which buildings are made....The challenge is to try to understand architectural practices as power-laden cultural practices that are deeply affected by larger historical forces, for instance, markets, the state, the academy, but also as practices that have their own specificity and social effects—even if they are not the kind of effects one approves of.[45]

Here are some positive examples where the market, the academy, and modernist isolating forces are not controlling the use and design of buildings and who decides. These are where West's concerns and Alexander's ideas about aliveness have come into being.

Dividend Housing

There's an ongoing conversation in many communities about afford- able housing. Most thinking treats the residents as needy, destined to move frequently, and indifferent to the care of the building they reside in. Private investors are a major beneficiary in developing af- fordable housing and most often retain ownership of the structure that they build. This means that what was funded with public money over time can be converted to market-rate housing.

There is one powerful innovation that has the capacity to turn that thinking on its head. In 2007, Margery Spinney decided that she was going to find a way to accomplish wealth creation for low-income people. Wealth creation for low-income people: that's quite a turn of phrase because most of us think low-income people are lacking something. Her innovation is now called Dividend Housing. Margery developed the nonprofit Cornerstone Corporation for Shared Equity, which introduced the concept of renter equity. With Carol Smith she cofounded Renting Partnerships, which addresses the horrors of eviction and wealth inequality by acquiring housing, keeping it in common ownership, and engaging residents to build wealth through participation in caring for the property.

Margery recruits low-income people as tenants in housing that her nonprofit owns and she manages. The management is what is unique. She engages the tenants as partners in the well-being of that building. They attend regular meetings, care for the grounds and hallways, and help in screening new tenants. By treating tenants as partners, tenants take care of the place, they stay longer, they take care of each other, and at the end of five years they've saved enough in the cost of managing the building that tenants receive $5,000 that they can use any way they want. If, during the five years, hardship occurs, tenants can borrow against their equity to pay rent. Low-income people are creating wealth simply by staying put and by the way they inhabit together the building in which they live. If we are looking for social innovations, this ranks near the top.

In Margery's words:

> Communal ownership of affordable housing that takes the land
> permanently off the market is critical. Residents have to feel
> that they can stay where they're living indefinitely. Not live in
> fear that the rent is going to go up or the building is going to be
> sold because the neighborhood is getting more valuable.
>
> What we are doing is shifting from a property-based economy
> to a relationship-based economy. It is a shift in mindset. From
> home ownership to housing security. I want to be secure where
> I live. I don't need to own it.[46]

Cohousing

Sarah Arthurs has been living in cohousing in Calgary with her family for years. She sees cohousing as an opportunity to bring people together as neighbors in a caring community. It's a substitute for gentrification and gives form to the common good. The concept of cohousing originated in Denmark in the late 1960s and is an intentional neighborhood with a small footprint. Cohousing can be townhouses in close proximity or an apartment building where everyone has a self-contained home and shares common space such as kitchen, dining room, lounge, and outdoor areas.

The benefits of cohousing are many—think of a village raising a child, a way to combat loneliness, how to enable older people to age in place, housing for the disabled or those with children who are disabled, and a multigenerational, extended family atmosphere. People agree to certain guidelines to join, and decisions are made by "refined con-sensus" (decisions that work for most of the people most of the time). They sign a mission and values statement. Everyone is part of a team (landscape, social, care, maintenance, technology). Some cohousing communities are formed by groups of people contributing money to purchase the land and buildings. Developers are now becoming inter-ested in financing cohousing units as an investment model.

"We have a living structure with people who have a different at-titude toward home ownership," Sarah says. "They want to live with other people that their children can play with.... You have community but you also have autonomy in deciding how you want to balance pri-vate time with cooperative effort."[47]

Hip-Hop Architecture

More than anyone, Robert Moses, as the head of a number of New York City's public works projects from the mid-1920s to the early 1960s, paved the way for the physical and cultural environment that encouraged the birth of hip-hop. In "The Fifth Pillar: A Case for Hip-Hop Architecture," Sekou Cooke observes that of the five pillars of Western culture—theater, music, dance, fine art, and architec-ture—four pillars find a parallel in hip-hop: DJing, emceeing, break dancing, and graffiti. The missing pillar is architecture, yet hip-hop would not be possible without urban settings and the accompany-ing architecture. Cooke's conclusion: "This fifth pillar will be built by, for, and upon the hip-hop generation."[48] It will have the qualities that speak to the eclectic and energized and to the social independence and critique that hip-hop expresses, combining several songs, beats, and street language into one creative piece of work.

Pocket Neighborhoods:
Making Space for Neighbor at the Center

The architect Ross Chapin has pioneered "pocket neighborhoods"—spaces that encourage conversation and community among neighbors. He uses porches and courtyards to allow people to engage with each other while maintaining a feeling of privacy in their homes. He talks about the importance of "place making" for the human soul and for the community. He explains: "While I focus in on the details of buildings and spaces and gardens, really my attention is how it affects our personal well-being and the relationships with those around us, including our nearby neighbors."[49]

Facing what he called the "tsunami of sprawl" in the 1960s and 1970s, Chapin began by teaming up with a developer to build an example of something that he thought would work to shift the trend. That development sold out immediately and the media picked the story up. Chapin's approach spread across the country and beyond very quickly. He says:

In much of the world that is being developed, houses are commodities. Houses are addresses. Houses have become investments rather than having a home be a place of belonging and a place of engagement with others. And in a bigger sense an engagement in democracy. We are essentially isolated and

we tie to the world through the car and through the Internet
now. And so I thought we can do something about that. We're
pretty isolated and I think we can come together again.[50]

Pocket neighborhoods provide a protected, intermediate zone that
is both public and private: there may be a common park, leading to a
fence, a front yard, a porch, then the front door. This design creates
a traffic-free environment for children's widening horizons. Chapin
believes this feature is critical for children, "to match their growing
curiosity and their need for increased responsibility for maturing
social skills." It also gives them other adults beyond their parents to
engage with as well as other children to play with in an unplanned
way.

Summing Up

We have listed only a few of the living and building arrangements that
exist within the common good narrative. There are church buildings
playing with space, like putting their kitchen and dining at the entrance to the building so you are welcomed by food instead of housing it and the women who usually cook it in the basement.

There are many places in architecture that pay close attention to
the common good and bringing citizens into contact with each other.
There are many architectural examples that support neighborliness
as the key concern, not only for how we build or redesign structures
but also how we design and occupy the interior of buildings—round
tables instead of rectangular ones, or chairs with wheels that sym-
bolize we can come together in a variety of ways. This is a form of

what we might call social architecture, which is the conscious design of ways we interact with each other inside spaces that support the common good.

America is a large friendly dog in a small room.

Every time it wags its tail, it knocks over a chair.

ARNOLD TOYNBEE

NINE

Common Good Protocols

Questions are fateful. They determine destinations.
They are the chamber through which destiny calls.

GODWIN HLATSHWAYO

As mentioned many times, a major impact of the business perspective and the consumer culture has been to outsource the solutions to our traditional collective concerns. Purchasing sugar at a convenience store instead of borrowing from a neighbor leaves us less interdependent and more disconnected from those around us. This has left behind modern neighborhoods that have become like a relational wilderness. Urban neighborhoods are too often described by their deficiencies. Rural places find their youth leaving town in the name of mobility and jobs.

Connection Precedes Content

The challenge in efforts to create an alternative future is the need for the effort to be sustainable. The path explored in this chapter shows ways to have citizens more powerfully connected to each other, especially those who were relative strangers up to now. Our traditional ways of doing this are to ask citizens to get involved by attending events as listeners, sending money, completing surveys, and writing letters. As a persuasive process, this approach builds support for the cause, but these activities are limited forms of engagement. The heavy lifting is done by people who launched the idea, or who are paid to do it or are heroic volunteers, and by institutions organized around a particular interest. The suggestion here is for us to put the heavy lifting in the hands of citizens. When we search for where the future exists in the present, we find it in the stories of citizens who are connected to each other in unique ways.

This chapter is about high impact ways to activate citizens, the methodology of relational activism. This is most often brought about by what we are calling common good protocols. To begin the discussion, we want to distinguish common good protocols from conventional business protocols or what might be considered royal protocols. Protocols are a set of rules and practices. The protocols of a dinner, for example, are often the sequence of appetizer, salad, entrée, dessert, and coffee. Salad later in some cultures. In our discussion here, we are considering specific structures of how we use our time when we come together.

Protocols in this sense are a way of repeated designs about how we gather and do things. For the common good, paying close attention to how we bring citizens together is not simply about how we hold a meeting. It is about how human beings join together to create a better world, which is accomplished through repeated designs about how we occupy the room together. These common good protocols are ways we create the conditions where reclaiming control of our collective well-being can be initiated and experienced at this moment.

This is what builds sustained effort. This is one way of thinking about how the common good gets activated.

Leadership Is Convening

When we commit to activating the common good, we know we need leadership. We just need leadership of a different kind than we are used to. Leadership that departs from the business perspective. Conventional leadership is needed when we seek control and predictability. This is leadership as cause and citizens, employees, and students as effect. We teach and are told that great leaders need to be role models. Have vision, be decisive, and give order and predictability to our world, be it a school system, a corporation, a church, a social service, or a city, state, or country.

As long as we keep the leader–follower relationship the center of our attention and training, our capacity to focus on citizens controlling their own well-being will remain an exception and a human-interest story. We have the expectation that business perspective leaders are in charge of not only the work to be done, but they are also central in shaping, guiding, and caring for the people they lead. In many ways we expect business perspective leaders to be good parents. We expect them to grow and develop "their" people. They "hold" people accountable, and they are where the buck stops.

A side effect of the traditional "strong leader" who is cause and at the center is that they leave citizens more polarized and divided. This is an inevitable outcome of leadership that feeds on the desire for certainty and safety. This form of leadership has much history on its side. When, around 1900, Frederick Taylor came along with time and motion studies, it was a step to have leaders manage "scientifically." This might make sense for a business. For situations where something is being manufactured. For maintaining the infrastructure of a city, building a bridge, or running a bank. But it is questionable even in a business but that is not the point here.

What is in question is what kind of leadership works best to activate and nurture the common good. Leadership serving the common good puts primary attention to the relationship between citizens, not to relationships between leaders and leaders or leaders and followers. This form of leadership helps citizens become relational activists and therefore accountable for fulfilling their concerns such as protecting the earth, the well-being of our children, or working toward social equity. When citizens are connected to each other, they will know how best to utilize help from the domains of social services, governments, faith communities, and business. Leadership serving the common good is in contrast to the traditional "strong leader" who is cause and becomes the center of attention and expectations.

Royal Protocols

One way to understand the leader's role from the business perspective is to lay out some of the protocols that have been created to reinforce our desire for order and control. They might be called royal protocols. When following protocols, it matters less who the leader is. There is little utility in blaming anyone. We can stop telling "truth to power," which is never powerful. The person is transcended by the protocols they choose to follow.

- One very common royal protocol is *Robert's Rules of Order*. Robert was an officer in the US Army who became dismayed at the chaotic way meetings occurred. He wrote his rules in 1876, and the book now is in its thirteenth edition. The order is old business, new business, reports, motions, seconds, discussion, vote, adjourn. All people in attendance are clearly grateful for an on-time ending.

- The concept of a board of directors is to provide oversight on how a system is being managed. The directors meet a few times a year to make sure the CEO or superintendent or executive director is doing the right thing. Another magical expectation of the patriarchal narrative is believing that outsiders can keep the train on track. Oversight takes many forms depending on the sector. Citizens watching the police. Activist investors calling for new leadership and tighter cost control.

- Performance reviews are annual events where the boss tells the subordinate how to improve their performance. The protocol has the boss mention positive comments, then negative comments, then positive comments. Sometimes called a "club" sandwich. The review is often enhanced by 360-degree anonymous feedback from coworkers adjacent to the person. It is a human resources–required event. No salary increases happen unless the review is held.

- The town hall meeting is another leader-loving ritual. Employees or constituents sit facing forward. The leader, with PowerPoints or not, delivers prepared comments, often written by a communications expert. Question-and-answer time is meant to respond to submitted written questions screened by staff to ensure no embarrassment.

- Other rituals include expert-based summits and conferences. Keynote speakers. Experts running workshops. These can be gatherings to improve a business, advocate for a cause, share knowledge about a field, or bring professionals and activists together to launch something new and special. The assumption is that knowledge can be acquired. Transmitted. As we will see, the biggest value from this royal way of convening is what happens between, before, and after the actual sessions.

- Hearings intended for citizen involvement have the officials on a platform with microphones. Citizens are given a few minutes to comment and move on. Board of education meetings are classic examples of a highly controlled structure to keep citizens contained.

- Any room with seating bolted to the floor is designed to elevate the speaker and neutralize the audience. Other facing-forward examples are classrooms, executive dining rooms, employee cafeterias, church sanctuaries, and courtrooms with elevated benches for the judge to rule from and an "all rise" when the judge enters the room. Another space designed for the ruling class is the boardroom, where the conference table rules. And let's not forget the aspirational front or corner office, on the top floor and, in one case I know of, a spiral staircase leading to heaven and the CEO.

It is important to say there are many businesses and organizations that have created different roles for their leaders. Circle-driven ways for citizens and employees to move things forward. In the 1980s employee involvement and quality circles were powerful and effective in having employees function as partners with management. Many churches have eliminated the pews and made the sanctuary a gathering place for people throughout the week. Some CEOs have left the corner office and sit near or next to the people doing the work. There are meeting spaces with round tables, open to all to use. Chairs with wheels.

The point is, these circle-driven ways are not typical. They have been proven to be effective, but are still rare.

Relational Activist

One of the most important functions for leaders is to support common good protocols that bring people together in a different way. This is the essence of the word *relational*. With these methods, common good leadership and activism is convening people in a way that puts our attention on citizen-to-citizen relationships. Whatever the interest or passion, we accelerate commitment by the way we gather in the moment. To achieve this and move from the pyramidal narrative of the business perspective, we need more radical engagement processes. These will encourage people to produce, with their neighbors, more ownership of the causes and functions they care most about.

A reason for naming common good leadership as a convening or hosting function is the need to make a cultural change from reinforcing dependency and compliance to reinforcing agency and accountability. This is where employees and citizens become cocreators of the future. By constructing a meeting room in order to foster peer or citizen connection and choosing the right questions to ask, we promote a spirit of equality. And partnership. The Industrial Age and the Information Age prioritize speed and productivity. The Age of Engagement and Convening prioritizes intimacy, commitment, and chosen accountability.

In the common good narrative, the role of leaders is to bring people together first and allow action plans and commitments to emerge. And to do this in a way that welcomes the stranger as a necessary source of surprise, be they someone new, someone who is upset, or someone from another culture. Leaders breaking people into small groups, asking questions, and saying "I don't know" invite mutual accountability. This way means the answer resides in the nature of the question. It is in sharp contrast to the desire to deliver certainty, a prime goal of the business narrative.

The small group is a vital element of an architecture for engagement. It is a relational version of Christopher Alexander's pattern language. For him, a balcony must be at least six feet wide. A pattern language for leaders is to break people into small groups of three, knowing this is the unit of transformation. Working in a small group is the pattern of assembly that encourages trusting others versus drawing back or competing with them. This also means that leaders do not need to hold the vision, be role models, and develop or train people.

Common good activism simply calls for leaders to construct the invitation, arrange the room, state the intention for the gathering, structure the moments or protocols, frame the question, and see that what is produced gets captured. Also to join the conversations as a participant. This is an alternative structure to the business protocols. It is not the absence of structure. The intent is to redesign leadership to take on the functions of connector, what we have traditionally called facilitator. This is a line management function, whether the convener is a boss, minister, politician, or service worker.

Common Good Protocols

These protocols serve the common good narrative. What they call for is twofold: (1) to give primary attention to building trust and voice among citizens, employees, neighbors, or whoever you are working with; and (2) to design a process where these players are central in choosing what to focus on and planning a path or plan that they themselves can act upon. This is distinct from a feedback loop for planners, designers, and managers to get a response to what they are thinking of doing. Just to be clear, this is not about consensus decision making. It is not about each person having a vote. Each may have a place, but they are not the point. Under common good protocols the point is about connection more than decision.

For example, for raising and educating a child, the parents focus on what we together can do to help their own or their neighbors' children grow and develop. They avoid conversations that focus on what the principal and teachers need to do differently. If we care about health, being part of local association life serves to minimize illness. If safety is the focus, the question is, what can we as neighbors do to clean up the neighborhood and keep eyes on the street to care for

one another's person and property? The point is not focusing so exclusively on what the police do. All professions and institutions are
needed in a crisis. The health-care industry is needed in the face of
disease. The fire department is needed when there is a fire. It is up to
citizens to be engaged with each other even when there is not a crisis.
The common good protocols are devices to make this happen.

About the Room

For the common good protocols to bring citizens together, we first
need to arrange the room in a specific way. Not complicated, just not
typical. The arrangement is in service of the quality of aliveness.

Ideally we need round tables. Or, when you feel brave, no tables—
just six chairs for each group arranged in a circle. Circles within two
feet of each other. This telegraphs to people upon entry that something new is coming. And that the room is configured so that they will
be talking to each other rather than being told, sold, guided, taught,
or entertained. When there are no tables, some people will complain
about where to put their things. What they are really saying is they
didn't come to be vulnerable or to share ignorance with other participants. Sympathize, have places around the edge of the room for
storage, and if some people want to sit near a table or face the front,
let them.

Next, you want everyone standing or sitting at the same level. As
convener, you stand on the same level as everyone else—no podium,
a microphone if needed. Open with a welcome. Offer a repeat of the
invitation and a restatement of the purpose of the gathering and how
the time will be structured. Within the first fifteen minutes, break

people into groups of three. Use the questions as described in the first protocol below and join a group.

That's it. No more interior design required. If you can't control the shape of the room, find a way to have three people talk to each other. I have run sessions in church sanctuaries and was stressed about what to do with people lined up in pews. Getting up my courage, I asked them to stand, find two other people they knew the least, and get a place to talk. They figured it out. Turned around in the pews, found the back of the room, sat on the steps to the altar. My caution was the issue, not the layout of the room.

Common Good Protocols in Action

This leads us to more detail about protocols that produce the connection and accountability that the common good depends on. We are naming several in this chapter that can be adapted. The point is to understand the ideas behind each protocol and customize. Some are done in groups of three, many in groups of six—it doesn't matter how many people are present. Six or six hundred, the protocol still works.

Conversational Domains for Activating Trust and Accountability

To change the culture, change the conversation. Werner Erhard introduced me to the concept of speech acts, which is the basis for the conversational protocols in this section. These domains hinge on a distinction between words that move the action forward versus just talk. "Just talk" includes opinions, persuasion, feedback, complaints, intellectual analyzing, explanations, excuses, naming people's deficiencies, the call for more research and planning, arguments, political points of view, appeasement, lip service—all the ways we detach from the present and the burden of being accountable, an agent. The advantage of these kinds of conversations or speech acts is they are interesting, rewarding, self-expressive, declare we are right, and imply steps to certainty. All a diversion from anything really changing. In terms of impacting the world, these conversations do not fulfill their promise and leave us with a sense of helplessness. Every time.

What we are seeking in creating a common good counternarrative is dialogue that moves the action forward. Dialogue where, in their very expression, the words chosen and said to one another produce accountability and agency *within* the speaker. And also, in the vulnerability of the expression, words that build trust with the other— the other being someone you might know the least, someone from a different culture, or someone with whom it has been difficult to be yourself.

Another word for accountability is *agency*, meaning the capacity to act. This is the antidote to helplessness. It is a vital dimension of the common good and in relational activism: engaging in conversations that mobilize citizens to join each other. This is what chosen accountability requires. Words that have the power to bring something new into being are declarations. Declarations of possibility. Or declarations in the extreme such as "I do," "You are under arrest," "You are hired," "You are fired," "We hold these truths to be self-evident." Or a sermon given on a mount.

Other more day-to-day words that are powerful speech acts are saying no; stating wants; making a request, commitment, promise, covenant, confession, agreement. Naming people's gifts. Offering forgiveness or declaring your unwillingness to do so. Each of these has choice embedded in the act. Each demands vulnerability on the part of the speaker. This is not a matter of semantics. Accountability and a declaration of our citizenhood are embedded in the statements themselves, regardless of the impact or how the world responds. There is the power to create an alternative future in the words themselves, the moment they are spoken, all through the vulnerability they invoke. And the choice is never an easy one. This is the essence of agency and social capital. When this is done as a collective, knowing all in the room are participating in the same conversation, the common good is activated.

Many of us have spent the last couple of decades, or centuries, discovering which conversational structures, triggered by certain questions, can evoke connection, even with strangers. One of several paths or protocols are the questions that follow. Answered in a group of three or four, they accelerate trust building, simply in the answering. We usually think creating trust takes time. With certain specifically worded questions and the right context, we can accelerate the process. Trust building among strangers or people we thought we knew takes three brief conversations, each under fifteen minutes. In most cases, no matter who is there, the room becomes a safer place than we had imagined possible. It means we are willing to discover whether there exists in this situation a longing to connect and an openness to the invitation. This is the belief behind this book's opening declaration that we are not divided.

We call the conversational domains that produce trust and accountability The Six Conversations.[51] These are more fully developed in my book *Community: The Structure of Belonging*. They are offered here in the context of protocols for the common good and one form of relational activism. More forms follow. In essence, these conversations are questions that, when offered in a nonjudging and non-helping context, produce an experience aligned with the deeper relational intent of the common good. They bring activism alive in the moment. This set of conversations, triggered by certain questions, are not six steps. Any one or two of them are all we need. We pick the conversations that fit the moment.

CONVERSATION ONE:
Invitation

Extend an invitation. Come. The invitation could be to a weekly meeting, a service, a learning, a coffee, book club, a council meeting, a discussion of your choice. It could be an invitation to a common concern such as safety, health, equity, schooling, the environment. Any effort to come together, including just to make things better. In the invitation is a statement of purpose and advance notice that this event will require you to join with other participants to explore your role in making something happen. The invitation is in contrast to a mandate or a sales pitch. It signals that something will be required of each of us. And that the purpose is something that you care about. No need to come out of obligation, to be an observer, to return a favor, or because someone talked you into it. These are all forms of relational passivism.

CONVERSATION TWO:
Possibility

This conversation has two parts: crossroads and possibility. The opening question is:

What is the crossroads you are at in this moment about something you care about? Your work, or this effort, this general concern, this budget, this neighborhood, this church, your life?

This question sets the stage for possibility. Asking about crossroads means that your life always contains a choice. The second question, usually answered near the end of the gathering, is:

What is the possibility that you can declare a stance for?

The possibility is a future condition that you believe in. It is not a goal. Not an outcome that you see a path to achieving. It is larger than these. It is something that you *hold*, not something that you *do*. When you are declaring a possibility, and do it in front of others, it means whenever you walk into a room, the possibility comes with you. Keep playing with the wording until saying it makes you uneasy.

CONVERSATION THREE:
Ownership

What is your contribution to having created the very thing that concerns you?

Tough conversation, tough question. If we cannot see our role in having created a problem, a disappointment, a pain, then *we* are treating ourselves as object, effect, victim. It means we have no course of action to make things better. This can be a relationship or something larger, like climate change or systemic racial inequality. If you really cannot see yourself as contributing, by omission or commission, then *that* stance, of being audience, is your contribution to the problem. There is no escape from accountability.

CONVERSATION FOUR:
Dissent

What doubts do you have about the path being considered or the ideas being offered?

Doubts need to be verbalized at every stage. If not spoken, they sap our energy. There is within the dissent discussion a series of questions that take us deeper into this conversation, each a step deeper into accountability.

What did you say "yes" to that you no longer mean?

It is difficult but important to acknowledge that we have changed our commitment. This is the antidote to excuses or talking about external events and their impact.

What is the "no" you have been postponing?

"No" is the beginning of a conversation of commitment. It acknowledges our humanity, which is to have ambivalence about anything that really counts.

CONVERSATION FIVE:
Commitment

What is the promise you are willing to make with no expectation of return?

No promise is an acceptable answer. This is an antidote to barter and entitlement. Both let us off the hook. A promise is the hook. Call it a covenant.

CONVERSATION SIX:

Gifts

What gifts have you received from others in this gathering? What gifts have you not yet fully brought into play?

The gifts conversation balances our passion for looking at what needs improvement. It signifies that we are enough. And gives voice to what we mean to each other. Gifts are the basis for the common good. They best take the form of being told to a person. Especially with witnesses.

These questions define a conversational domain of relational activism. Every time we address any one of these conversations, we create the conditions for building trust and activating the common good. None of these questions are perfect or clear. That is the point. Each asks us to be vulnerable. We can keep returning to a question and it will have new meaning and depth each time. The point is to initiate conversations that evoke accountability in each other's presence. Citizen to citizen. This is the relational requirement to realizing the common good and making it central to our lives. They, along with the other protocols, are the necessary conditions for taking control of our collective well-being.

Open Space: Who Decides What Matters?

Another common good protocol for engaging citizens as agents is called Open Space Technology, developed by Harrison Owen. It is another pattern for partnership, convening, and shared ownership. Instead of an agenda, an outcome, and a path to get there, this structure or protocol begins with a general question related to why the gathering was called and asks participants to nominate ideas to pursue. They then convene a conversation with other participants who are also interested in a particular idea.

Harrison understood that what typically happens in the room or the hallway during breaks, or before and after an event, is that we engage in casual conversations that are as worthwhile as the main event. Open Space creates a language and simple set of protocols to have the experience of those "in-between" points of contact be the actual structured way we meet. Virtual or live, it shifts the experience of being together. In Harrison's words the inspiration started in West Africa:

> I had this image from my days in West Africa of how people start a useful discussion. They sit in a circle. You don't have to yell at them. You don't have to organize them. You don't have to do a thing. They sit in a circle. And sitting in a circle was a good place to start, but what are we going to talk about? And the image of a bulletin board appeared in my mind. And it's true all over the world, you want to buy something, sell something, complain about something, you put it on a bulletin board.

> So I thought, "Right, well, we'll just tack stuff up on the wall and make a bulletin board." So now we're all together. We know what we want to talk about. And all we've got is the logistics, who, where, when, and how. And the image that came to my mind was a marketplace, an indigenous marketplace. And the wonderful part about that is they happen. Nobody organizes them. Nobody controls them. But they happen. And ideas and

goods and everything else get exchanged. And at that point, the gin ran out. But that's Open Space. Sit in a circle, create a bulletin board, open a marketplace, go to work.[52]

Here is the way it works in a live gathering. It can work from six to several hundred at a time. This is not the whole process but gives a feel for the structure:

1. The convener comes up with a question. Examples: How do we reduce late arrivals in the classroom? How do we eliminate the drug traffic in our neighborhood? How to reduce response time when our servers are down? Is there a God? (A question President Eisenhower asked an early mainframe computer in the 1950s. He got an answer: "There is now!")

2. On the wall are lists of times and places for small group meetings to occur in a few minutes.

3. Participants are each given a blank sheet of paper and a marker and a piece of tape.

4. They are given ten minutes to identify the conversation they would like to host related to the main question and write it on the sheet of paper. Each is free to list a conversation or not. They post the paper on the wall under a time and place.

5. Then participants decide which conversation they want to join. They go to that place. The meetings will last one hour. There can be more than one round of meetings depending on overall time. And, if a host who put a subject on the wall sees a discussion they would rather attend, they can go

there. The protocol is meticulous in offering choice in a variety of small ways. This is what provides the quality of aliveness Christopher Alexander talks about. It is a version of Jane Jacobs's earlier quote that "sidewalk contacts are the small change of which the wealth of public life may grow."

6.   When the groups meet, one person agrees to take notes and report back to the general session when all reconvene. They turn in their notes to the convener. Then a second round begins.

7.   The final general session discusses what has been learned and how to move forward.

Here are some general guidelines pioneered by Harrison.[53] These four principles can be applied to all we do.

1.   Whoever comes to the meeting are the right people.

2.   Wherever and whenever it happens is the right place.

3.   When a meeting is over, it's over.

4.   Law of Two Feet: If you find yourself in a place where you're not learning or contributing, use your two feet and go somewhere else where you can.[54]

World Café: Wiser Together

Juanita Brown, creator of the World Café, said that every act is a mixture of metaphor and methodology. Everything you do, every step, is an act in itself and also a metaphor, an approximation or symbol of how to involve people in a way that demonstrates how we want the larger world to function. That means that no act or event is too small to make a difference. If you desire scale, it always begins with words and a manageable event. The construction of each step declares that we are in the business of being intentional designers of an experience of the commons.

Using the Café's words: "People already have within them the wisdom and creativity to confront even the most difficult challenges; the answers we need are available to us, and we are Wiser Together than we are alone."[55]

Here is the basic World Café protocol at a glance. Just to give you a feel for the process and see its power. The patterns:

- Seat five people at a small café-style table or in small group clusters. Have as many tables as needed to seat everyone.

- Set up at least three rounds with people changing tables after twenty minutes. One person stays put.

- Provide one or more questions related to why the event was organized.

- Encourage people to chat and write and doodle on paper on the table or on notecards if there are no tables.

- The moving around cross-pollinates the ideas and connections in the room.

- At the end, people come together to share insights and discoveries. And talk of possibilities for action.

Like all of these common good protocols and more that follow, these processes invert our traditional thinking about where the expertise lies and where actions and accountability reside. These are the mobilizing essence of the common good, whether in a gathering, a neighborhood, or an organization. It is where passion for a question and convening for action intersect. This is the alternative to the royal protocols of summits, town hall meetings, city council hearings, bringing community in for feedback.

The Art of Hosting

The art of hosting is another common good protocol for engaging people across all boundaries and levels and stories. It is yet one more design for the affirmation of the gifts of each person. The art of hosting is organized around a question, as are all common good protocols. The question is open-ended with no clear direction. The questions are what the hosting team considers important for our future well-being. Some examples are what is needed to make this neighborhood safer, to have this work be more efficient, to make the city more welcoming.

The art of hosting has its own particulars:

- A host who named the question and made the invitation.
- A circle guardian who cares for the energy, timing, verbosity, sequence, and balancing of the conversation. This person also decides when whole group and small group work is appropriate. This allows the host to join as a full participant.
- A talking stick passed around to ensure all voices are heard.
- Harvesters who track and record what comes out of the circle conversations. These records can be posted, typed, or simply verbally summarized.[56]

The intent of this protocol is to hear people's voices and see where there is convergence. It also defines what are the ideas and steps where we choose to come together to take action and sort out responsibilities and commitments. This aspect echoes the business perspective, but the common good protocol takes the time and patience to allow and require citizens and participants to have their fingerprints on the product throughout. This builds social capital so energy is sustainable. It also reduces the need to sell the changes to those most affected.

The Art of Convening

Few people have refined the process of bringing people together as clearly as Craig and Patricia Neal. Their Art of Convening is really the art of leading in our terms here.[57] The core of this method is the Convening Wheel, which brings together the practices and principles needed for authentic engagement. Some of the key parts of their way of gathering and engaging is detailed in a wheel as follows:

- **At the heart of the matter.** Who I am in relationship with others.

- **Clarifying intent.** The alignment of our intention with the purpose of our engagement.

- **The Invitation.** A sincere offering to engage that integrates larger purpose and this gathering.

- **Setting context.** Communicating the form, function, and purpose of our engagement and intent.

- **Creation**. Something new that emerges from engagements of shared purpose and trust.

- **Commitment to action**. An individual and/or collective agreement to be responsible and accountable for the way forward.[58]

All five of the common good protocols fit easily with each other. And there are many more, each with its own nuances. Each begins with peer-focused convening and commitment. After that, it may be time to engage experts and institutions as a second or third wave of participation. Each of these protocols can also occur in a room with hundreds of people. These forms of gathering and engaging are really forms of relational activism as we are using the term. They call leadership to three tasks:

1. Create a context that nurtures a future based on gifts, generosity, accountability, and commitment.

2. Initiate and convene conversations that shift people's experience, which occurs through the way they are brought together and the nature of the questions used to engage them.

3. Design the moment so as to have participants' way of speaking and listening and connecting with each other the first priority. There will be plenty of time for traditional content and planning, for this is the information age, just a click away.

Summing Up

Relational activism is based on a form of activism and leadership that creates processes in which more are heard, profound exchanges take place, and choices are made. The common good leadership protocols are the concrete expression of what is underlying the social innovations highlighted throughout this book. Christopher Alexander did it for architecture. Mike Mather for religion. Mark Anielski is doing it for measures of well-being. Mike Butler did it for offenders. And, as you will see in the next chapter, Jeff Yost is doing it for philanthropy. Ann Livingston for addicts. These and more are examples of activating the common good. And taking an active step toward making both our beliefs and our way of coming together different from what we normally have expected to occur—that is, the business perspective.

Maybe the purpose of problem solving is to give us an excuse to work together, rather than the opposite, which is the only reason we work together is to problem solve.

JIM KEENE

TEN

The Neighborhood

The village beats the bank. Villagers bear witness
of the power of life that occurs as the alternative
to royal protocol and the power of sales and
marketing masquerading as explanation.

WALTER BRUEGGEMANN

The neighborhood is the landing spot for creating a culture that shifts us away from being commodities at work and consumers at home. The neighborhood is where major shifts toward the common good occur. It is the venue within reach where we reclaim control of our collective well-being. The neighborhood is about place and memory and a way of being together with our shared interests providing the excuse.

Neighborhoods are not the whole story for the common good, they are just where the common good is most accessible. They are the delivery system for the common good as we are using the term in this book. The neighborhood is surely not the only venue. Concerns about education, the environment, safety, health care, economics, social equity, and isolation transcend any particular place. There are national and global movements. The efforts in producing real broad-scale change in these dimensions are well populated and still need our attention and effort. Our concern in this moment is what is close at hand, believing that when people become active in controlling their more local well-being, their commitment to the larger movements is accelerated.

Genuine Wealth

Some years ago, I was invited to a conference of economists and for two days I was dazzled. People were telling me things that I just didn't know. Thank you, John Cobb and Ellen Brown, for your commitment to public banks. I didn't know that there was a state bank in North Dakota that avoided the highs and lows of economic cycles by creating money outside the private banking system. I didn't know that the national debt is mostly interest that we pay to the private sector. I was not aware of the extent to which debt matters to all of us.

I was invited to this conference by economist Mark Anielski, who focuses on an economy of well-being and happiness. He thinks that this is so important today because we are on the verge of many significant shifts in the world system. In addition to climate change, he says we are on the verge of a significant debt crisis that we will all soon be a part of and it will be worse than 2008. He questions why, just since World War II, we have continued to measure progress using tools like the Gross Domestic Product and standard-of-living measures. Mark believes we have an obligation to reestablish a deeper understanding of the word *economy*, which means helpful, stewarding, household management.

As Mark explains it:

I call our current economy a form of debt slavery and to free us from that would mean to re-orient our economy, which I am calling an economy of well-being. That economy should be built on what I call Genuine Wealth, the word meaning the conditions of well-being from the Old English and the word happiness meaning spiritual well-being from the Greek.

The province of Alberta is focused on the theme of health and wellness. They asked me, how are you measuring wellness? I said that we are going into communities and neighborhoods and talking to our neighbors about what brings their life meaning. What are their gifts and skills? Asking them their subjective opinions about their expectations of their well-being for themselves, for their work and for their children. Then marrying that with objective metrics that we collect regularly anyway. We collect all kinds of social economics statistics and health statistics. We need to marry the experiential information of the self-ratings of well-being with the objective data.[59]

In addition to Mark converting market and business focus into a common good measure, there are a variety of dimensions that are all needed to build our capacity to provide our common good. Keeping the circulation of money local. Sustaining local enterprise, community banking, real human wealth measured by social capital, schools that work for all kids, communally owned land and spaces—all are about productive neighborhoods. The common good occurs when we communally own local land and end the incentives for displacing residents for real estate development. For journalism, the neighborhood provides the stories for the reconstitution of the news. It is where journalism might decide that small and nearby surprises are news.

Restoring the Functions of Neighborhoods

We are considering well-being in terms of certain functions that every neighborhood or rural town needs to perform. The question is whether citizens have control over these functions or expect them to be handled by professionals and institutions. This is not a criticism of the professionals or institutions. It is the primary role they have been asked to play. And when we outsource accountability that rightfully belongs under our own leadership and direction, we are active participants in extinguishing social capital. We pay an especially high price since social capital is at the heart of caring for the earth, our children, our safety, our health, and the reality of loneliness.

The neighborhood is where every citizen can become an active player in creating more balance between what we produce with each other and what is produced by professionals and global commerce. As Wendell Berry sees it: "A viable community, like a viable farm, protects its own production capacities. It does not import products that it can produce for itself. And it does not export local products until local needs have been met. The economic products of a viable community are understood either as belonging to the community's subsistence or as surplus, and only the surplus is considered to be marketable abroad."[60]

Still, rebuilding the vitality of the neighborhood to produce its own well-being is a difficult task. It is likely to require youth and teenagers to bring their time and gifts to bear. It will require restoring to them a function and skills and value that disappeared in the move to the suburbs and the urge to keep them occupied, off the streets, and safe. For our concern for safety, it calls for neighbors to keep their eyes and feet on the street and to know their neighbors regardless of their potentially different-than-ours points of view.

Below are some of the most innovative, local, citizen-based efforts to put our lives in our own hands, which is the essence of what creates a living democracy and embodies the fact that we are not divided. What these efforts have in common is that they are small scale, slow to emerge, dependent on neighbors, and not well funded. Some are also examples of where institutions can launch and support citizen accountability through their convening function.

Putting "Neighbor" at the Center

DeAmon Harges has the official title of Roving Listener in his diverse neighborhood in Indianapolis, Indiana. He started as the first Roving Listener with Mike Mather (mentioned in chapter six). When the church moved from programs to discovering the gifts of its neighbors, DeAmon was the first one knocking on doors. Now, as a founder of the Learning Tree, an association of neighbors working to improve the quality of lives of people, schools, and businesses, DeAmon gathers people together to discover their gifts and talents in a systematic way.

People who live in the area open their doors to DeAmon when he introduces himself as a neighbor. He witnesses what they are already doing, allowing their invisible contributions to become visible. Regular celebration is an important aspect of building trust. Neighbors gain social capital through community parties to which they invite outside groups like the police, bankers, philanthropists, and city leaders. There are thriving food production, distribution, and catering enterprises in this neighborhood. Regular festivals are held that promote local artists and bring neighborhood crafts and skills together, operating like a local trade association.

DeAmon and his team organize all of this. They organize it by the way they gather people, by what we are calling relational activism. They lead by convening and hosting. His neighborhood and others like it are full of life, philanthropy, art, energy, culture, and history—mostly ignored by the dominant culture of the social service and business narrative.

Here are DeAmon's own words on how simple and profound the work can be: "Roving Listener [means] I'm a person who kidnaps other people to throw them on one another....I discover the gifts and talents of everyone in our community. Find a place for those gifts, celebrate those gifts, and make those gifts utilized in ways that will create a community economy and mutual delight."[61] In this neighborhood and ones like it, which we misname for many reasons, there is aliveness. This is the common good in plain sight. DeAmon has created both the narrative that fits his work and ways to bring funding that stays under neighbor and citizen control. He is making this common good model nationally visible by documenting what is occurring and creating interest among national news groups. This is one clear picture of the future.

A Health Authority

Another example of local people taking charge of their well-being comes from Chicago via Jackie Reed. Jackie grew up in the American South with a strong sense of family and community. Working in Chicago, she saw programs actively seeking to get people on welfare, along with a breakdown in the morals and values she was raised with. Neighborhoods were missing a sense of identity and purpose. As a social worker, Jackie was hired to work at a local church as their director of community health. Through that experience, it became obvious that community and social isolation, not health problems, were the issue.

As Jackie explains it, the standard approach was to attempt to fix people's problems for them. People lost their sense of what they could do for themselves and the difference they could make in their community. Jackie started the Westside Health Authority and began asking those in the community what they thought would make their neighborhoods healthier. Answers came back: address violence, provide more jobs and local businesses, affirm morals and values. Her Health Authority found hospitals that provided paid internships for young people to learn a multitude of skills, bringing hope and respect. The hospitals began using local businesses for the things they normally outsourced to larger companies. Jackie and her team started Every Block a Village (EBV) and found a citizen-leader on each block who would build relationships with neighbors and foster neighbors helping neighbors. Turns out the biggest health issue is hopelessness.

Neighborhood Advocate

Another example of neighbors taking charge of their well-being is in Tarrant County, Texas. Since 1992, Youth Advocate Programs (YAP) has been successfully providing a neighborhood-based alternative to sending juveniles into correctional institutions. A key to the program is pairing the young person with an advocate from the same zip code to codevelop and execute a plan that supports the family and brings in resources uniquely designed for their own situation. The first year of the county's program saw a 44 percent reduction in crime, which has been sustained. Gary Ivory, senior executive officer and national director of program development for Youth Advocate Programs, Inc., which runs in twenty-four states, tells the story:

> [In 1992] I moved back to my home state of Texas. Tarrant County, at the time, had one of the highest homicide and juvenile crime rates in the country.... They brought us in to do work in some of the areas of Tarrant County where the mail was not even being delivered; some of those neighborhoods were so violent.

> [We started] a neighborhood-based recruitment of residents. We call them advocates.... We had a mandate that we wouldn't hire an advocate unless they were from the same neighborhood where the kids who were being referred to the probation department came from.

> The credentials that we're looking for are compassion, unconditional love, self-forgiveness and forgiveness of others, the willingness to not judge people based upon their history or their offense.

Tarrant County, for over 20 years, has had the lowest
commitment rates to the Texas Juvenile Justice Department,
which simply means that we're solving problems in the
neighborhoods versus committing them to correctional
institutions.

You might ask why isn't this in every neighborhood? Part of it is,
nobody considers this a news story. The news consumes itself
with violence, but it does not consider saving a life worthy of
news unless a fireman does it at the top of a ladder.[62]

The Nebraska Community Foundation

Here is an example where home-grown initiative, including funding,
is being convened to create ways enterprise, education, and capital
are growing from local cooperation. This represents an alternative to
philanthropy operating under the business perspective. It's radical in
spirit and restorative in form.

Economist Jeff Yost works for the Nebraska Community Foundation as it strives to shape the future of rural communities affected by
the great outmigration of wealth. Nebraska Community Foundation
is not a charity but is a partner to community leaders to help them
retain wealth and resources. Due to population shifts—younger people moving from small towns to large urban areas and aging demo-
graphics—the transfer of wealth between generations goes where
the younger generation locates. Too often this means leaving town.

The Foundation only works with locally raised funds. It meets with
leaders of these affected smaller communities to help them with

goal setting and planning. If just 5 percent of the wealth that leaves a community is given back to the place where it was created, there would be a perpetual income stream to benefit that area. The community itself decides where this money is best spent, so the effort is community-driven. The Foundation functions as an investment manager of the local funds, offering education and training through peer-to-peer learning. You can see in his thinking how his function is to actively bring people together to control their future.

As Jeff explains it:

> The goal is to focus on having community leaders and citizens really be in conversation with one another. I am absolutely of the opinion that people hear something differently from a peer than they do from someone who is professionalized and being paid for doing that work. So, a tremendous amount of our training and education is actually done within the context of peer learning and peer mentoring.

> The interesting thing about using philanthropy as a community development tool is that you can't make anybody do anything. So, much of what we do is to help community leaders to become comfortable and confident to be able to talk to their friends, neighbors, and people that they have deep trusting relationships with about what is the difference that they each could make in the future of their town.[63]

Communities that are doing really well in this work are those that are figuring out how to engage dozens and hundreds of their neighbors in conversations about the future of their place and inviting them to be a part of that. "Our work is to help people really focus on the future," Jeff says, "and focus on what are the things that help to build and ultimately magnetize this community. So young people will say, this is where I want to live and work. This is where I want to raise my family. Where I want to have my business."[64]

Organizing the Un-organizables

Ann Livingston organizes drug users in Vancouver, British Columbia. When she moved into the neighborhood in 1993, she asked a basic question: "What should we do when someone is destitute and on the street and has reached their low ebb?" Ann observed that social services, the health department, the police, the court system, service organizations—all seemed disconnected and often worked at cross-purposes.

Ann works with addicted individuals to improve their lives and not just remove them from the community. Initially she invited them into her home, listened to them, and challenged them to action by coming together and forming an association. They rented a storefront where drug users could drop in. It became an unofficial safe injection site. She cofounded an organization now known as VANDU (Vancouver Area Network of Drug Users) that has a local and national impact. Their mission states that they are a group of users and former users who work to improve the health and well-being of those who use drugs. Ann has used principles of organizing to give structure to the organization. Weekly meetings are held where users can share what is really happening in their lives. Guest speakers come to address some of the questions addicts have about patient rights, social services, and legal issues. Belonging to this group has been a compelling motivator for people who are not welcome elsewhere.

As the organization has grown, the groups have specialized and are comprised of people living with similar addictions. VANDU members have expanded their focus to include community work, advocacy, and education, and they are engaging as citizens in their neighborhoods. One example is an urban park that they make sure is well cared for. Ann commented in a recent conversation:

> I was reminded of a study where they take these unhealthy people who smoke and drink and eat too much, in two communities. One has a high amount of community associations and activities, and the other one doesn't. Well, everyone with strong associational life lives longer, but it isn't because they improved their health habits. It was their support and social capital that had health consequences. I don't end up knowing very much about drugs, other than by accident; I do know something about bringing people together.
>
> One of the things that drug users do all day long, every day, is talk about drugs. In VANDU, they don't talk about that. They talk about the next meeting. How's our funding? What's going to be the topic, and who's going to be the guest speaker? Who's taking the trip to Ottawa? Who's coming here? Who is going to care for the park in our neighborhood?[65]

It is a longer story, but one simple and profound outcome was that annual deaths from drug use were cut in half. I was stunned. I asked Ann if her efforts had also reduced addiction among the users. She said she never asked that question. She accepted them for who they are.

Social Determinants of Health

Another example of neighborhoods at work comes from Deborah Puntenney. She works with the Greater Rochester Health Foundation (GRHF), which is interested in the social determinants of health and awards grants to local communities. Grantees are neighborhood groups. They are not meant to deliver programs or services; the groups are funded to organize their communities around neighborhood improvements they want to see. Even though it is a health foundation, it spends the first years bringing neighbors together to decide what they want to do to make things better where they live.

Deborah describes some of the impact of the foundation's work:

> There's been massive community change in this area....They
> absolutely understand how entrenched the issues are in
> terms of the social determinants of health, at least in terms
> of how they function in a negative way. And they sort of built
> backwards from the health outcome we seek. If we're hoping
> for long-term improvements in the incidence of, say, stroke or
> diabetes in these neighborhoods, we have to really think clearly
> about how to build their connection with each other and how
> long that's going to take.
>
> There are a lot of foundations who use the buzzwords:
> community, local. But they don't really, really indicate through
> their requirements that they trust people to actually make a
> difference in this regard.
>
> They encourage partnership, but generally it's a top-down
> kind of thing where the people who are the experts, the

professionals, are in the position of trying to get residents
to partner with them. As opposed to what we're trying to do,
which is to have the residents inviting agencies and institutions
to partner with them.[66]

This approach has affirmed that health is not fundamentally determined by the health-care industry. Another equally powerful insight was their appreciation that local people are the knowledgeable people. And that the social capital in their community is their resource base. They also are patient, thinking in terms of a decade to make a difference.

A Center for Hip-Hop and Respect

Elementz is an urban arts center in Cincinnati, Ohio, focusing on hip-hop, dance, and graffiti. It grew out of a protest against the police that turned into a street uprising in 2001. A group of people in their twenties wanted to do something in response to the outcry. They tried a cop watch but quickly saw how futile that was. Under the leadership of Gavin Leonard, they began to ask youth in the inner city what they really cared about. The answer was overwhelmingly hip-hop. Out of this they created an arts center where fourteen- to twenty-four-year-old urban youth—the age group many people are uneasy about—could learn to compose, record, perform, lay down beats, engineer, and do everything else involved in creating, DJing, and delivering hip-hop music. They soon added dance, poetry, and street art. Graffiti was now an art form on canvas rather than on trains and buildings.

What is unique is the program only focuses on the gifts of the youth. They never ask whether they are in school, active in the street or drug culture, have a record with the police, or where they are sleeping these days. Youths can become a member of Elementz for ten dollars a year, paid in installments. When you join, you sign up for classes and the studios are available to you. Twenty years into it, the youth perform more than two hundred times a year in schools, with the symphony and ballet, and at other public events.

One thing learned at Elementz was that when youth first show up, they are asked how many adults have their interests at heart. The answer for many young folks is one or two. For some of them it is none. When asked again after six months, the answer grows to four or five from their involvement with the center, and the young people tend to return to school and pull back from street culture. All without any urging or coaching or mentoring by Elementz. Through the years there have been the usual difficulties and hard times inherent with closely engaging with the drama sometimes facing this population. Elementz stays unique in that they do not have something in mind for the youth. Their goal is simply to create a vehicle for African American youth to be valued for what they already care about. And through that they discover their capacity to learn, to be creative, and to be productive.

Abundant Community Initiative

A final example is from the city of Edmonton, Alberta, where Howard Lawrence began an Abundant Community Initiative with the sponsorship of the city. The initiative is unique in the way that government has invested in citizens without having an answer in mind. This initiative is organized so that a neighbor or two will initiate a casual conversation with each household on their block about what activities and interests they care about as well as the gifts and abilities they are willing to share with their neighbors. This has reached the scale of fifty block connectors organizing conversations and connections. They have also developed a series of tools and common good protocols to allow this to spread throughout the city. The Edmonton initiative is a strong example of a traditional institution, government, convening citizens to be directly involved in producing their own well-being.

Finally

In all of these examples the common good is given voice by the creative and prophetic side of our lives. The strength of a local culture is sustained and informed every time we gather to participate in neighborhood efforts. This can be through food, language, stories, gardens, irritation, block parties, live entertainment in a home, or cleaning up Ludlow Avenue. These stories also focus on neighborhood gifts, philanthropy, youth offenders, addiction, health, and hip-hop art, which are only a few of the social innovations that surround us. What these examples—and others sprinkled throughout this book—have in common is that each is locally focused and begins with the capacities of citizens to decide on and control issues they care about.

Relational activism is an invitation for citizens to become active in developing and producing the common good. It is also meant to highlight the shift in story about who we are. And to focus on a few fields of interest that are moving toward this narrative shift: journalism, architecture, and religion. A few examples of what form this takes in the world of action have been offered. There are many more, but I did not want to add too many pages to the book by listing them. More examples are available on our website restorecommons.com and in Bollier's *Commoner's Catalog for Changemaking* and the work of Jay Walljasper.

The fact that each example is organized around the gifts and capacities of local citizens is what puts the "good" in the common good, as a counterstory to the business perspective, where goods and services are items to be purchased. The common good is activated by gathering around a set of communal protocols and questions that evoke what citizens can create with the capacities they currently hold, a process that produces citizen accountability, activating citizenship beyond voting. This strategy begins with recognizing that active citizens trusting each other first, then focusing on talents and producing their own future and narrative, is what serves the common good. This is activating the common good. This is the means through which we reclaim control of our well-being.

Thanks for stopping by.

As Robert Frost did not say,

"If you come to a fork in the road, take it."

NOTES

We Are Not Divided

1. "Common good" in *Oxford English Dictionary Online*.
2. Moyer, "Four Roles of Social Activism."
3. McKnight, "Neighborhood Necessities."

One: Taking Care of Business

4. Berry, *What Matters?*, 20.

Two: The Common Good Perspective

5. Rowe, *Our Common Wealth*, 29.
6. Cahn, "What Is TimeBanking?"

Three: The Business Perspective

7. Lovins et al., *Finer Future*, 39–30.
8. Lovins et al., *Finer Future*, 51.
9. Wood, *Origins of Capitalism*, 2.
10. Wood, *Origins of Capitalism*, 23.
11. Muller, *Mind and the Market*, 322–323.
12. Peter Block and Walter Brueggemann, personal correspondence.
13. Sale, *Rebels against the Future*, 28–29, emphasis in original.
14. Gunja, Gumas, and Williams, "U.S. Health Care from a Global Perspective, 2022."

Four: Distinctions for the Common Good

15. Patel, *Value of Nothing*, 23.

Five: A Just Economy

16. powell, "Poverty and Race through a Belongingness Lens."
17. Lynch, "Rethinking Racism."
18. Frazier, "A 'New Direction.'"
19. Berman, *All That Is Solid Melts into Air*, 62–69.
20. Whitfield, "We Don't Need Butter, We Need the Cow."
21. Whitfield, "We Don't Need Butter, We Need the Cow."
22. Clark, "Visions of a Just Economy."

Six: Religion beyond Boundaries

23. See, e.g., Lupton, *Toxic Charity*; and Villanueva, *Decolonizing Wealth*.
24. Loy, *Buddhist History of the West*, 197.
25. Loy, "Religion of the Market."
26. Mather, "From Charity to Empowerment."
27. Mather, "From Charity to Empowerment."
28. Mather, "From Charity to Empowerment."
29. Conboy, "Place at the Table."
30. Conboy, "Place at the Table."
31. Father Joe and Peter Block, personal correspondence.
32. Kovitch, "Church Turned Inside Out."
33. Kovitch, "Church Turned Inside Out."
34. Terlinchamp, "Radical and Freeing Work of Enacting Jubilee."

Seven: Journalism of What Matters and What Works

35. Cornuelle, "Our One-Eyed Press," 35–39.
36. Ehrlichman, quoted in Baum. "Legalize It All."
37. Bridges, "Social Psychology Behind Fake News."
38. Butler, "Ensuring Public Safety in a Sustainable Way."
39. Abello, "Prove Me Wrong," e-mail to Peter Block, May 4, 2022.
40. Pearlman, "Journalism with Community at the Center."
41. Pearlman et al., "Dialogue Journalism Toolkit."
42. Ellis, "New Ways to Tell the News."
43. Holman, "An Open Letter to Journalists."

Eight: Architecture of Aliveness

44. Alexander, *Timeless Way of Building*, 101.
45. West, *Keeping Faith*, 40, 42.
46. Spinney, "Financing a New Housing Paradigm."
47. Arthurs, "Intentional Neighborhoods in Co-Housing."
48. Cooke, "The Fifth Pillar."
49. Chapin, "Making Space for Community."
50. Chapin, "Making Space for Community."

Nine: Common Good Protocols

51. The Six Conversations were first introduced in my book *Community*, 113–143.
52. "Harrison Owen on Open Space."
53. "Harrison Owen on Open Space."
54. Owen, *Open Space Technology*, 92–96.
55. Brown and Isaacs, *World Café*, 4.
56. The full name of this protocol is "The Art of Hosting and Harvesting Conversations That Matter," https://artofhosting.org/.
57. Neal, Neal, and Wold, *Art of Convening*.
58. Neal, Neal, and Wold, *Art of Convening*, 7–9.

Ten: The Neighborhood

59. Anielski, "Meaning of Genuine Wealth."
60. Berry, *What Matters?*, 192.
61. Harges, "Neighborhood Is the Center."
62. Ivory, "Organizing Residents to Solve an Impossible Challenge."
63. Yost, "Hometown of Your Dreams."
64. Yost, "Hometown of Your Dreams."
65. Livingston, "Organizing the Un-organizables."
66. Puntenney, "How Community Action Shapes Health."

BIBLIOGRAPHY

Alexander, Christopher, et al. *A Pattern Language: Towns, Buildings, Construction.* New York: Oxford University Press, 1977.

———. *The Timeless Way of Building.* Center for Environmental Structure. New York: Oxford University Press, 1979.

Anielski, Mark. *An Economy of Well-Being: Common-Sense Tools for Building Genuine Wealth and Happiness.* Gabriola Island, BC: New Society Publishers, 2018.

———. "The Meaning of Genuine Wealth." *Restore Commons*, January 12, 2017. https://www.restorecommons.com/the-meaning-of-genuine -wealth/.

Arthurs, Sarah. "Intentional Neighborhoods in Co-Housing." *Restore Commons*, September 30, 2019. https://www.restorecommons.com /intentional-neighborhoods-in-co-housing/.

Baum, Dan. "Legalize It All." *Harper's Magazine* (April 2016): 22–32. https:// harpers.org/archive/2016/04/legalize-it-all/.

Berman, Marshall. *All That Is Solid Melts into Air: The Experience of Modernity.* New York: Penguin Books, 1988. Reissue edition, London: Verso, 2010.

Berry, Wendell. *The Gift of Good Land: Further Essays Cultural and Agricultural*. Berkeley, CA: Counterpoint, 1981.

———. *The Unsettling of America: Culture & Agriculture*. Reprint, Berkeley, CA: Counterpoint, 2015.

———. *What Matters?: Economics for a Renewed Commonwealth*. Berkeley, CA: Counterpoint, 2010.

Block, Peter. *Community: The Structure of Belonging*. 2nd edition. Oakland, CA: Berrett-Koehler, 2018.

Block, Peter, Walter Brueggemann, and John McKnight. *An Other Kingdom: Departing the Consumer Culture*. Hoboken, NJ: John Wiley & Sons, 2016.

Bollier, David. *The Commoner's Catalog for Changemaking: Tools for the Transitions Ahead*. Great Barrington, MA: Schumacher Center for a New Economics, 2021.

———. *Think Like a Commoner: A Short Introduction to the Life of the Commons*. Gabriola Island, BC: New Society Publishers, 2017.

Bollier, David, and Silke Helfrich. *Free, Fair and Alive: The Insurgent Power of the Commons*. Gabriola Island, BC: New Society Publishers, 2019.

———. *Patterns of Commoning*. Amherst, MA: The Commons Strategies Group in cooperation with Off the Common Books, 2015.

Bridges, Tristan. "The Social Psychology Behind Fake News." *HuffPost*, February 27 and March 2, 2017. https://www.huffpost.com/entry/why -the-american-public-seems-allergic-to-facts_b_58b4e9b6e4b02 f3f81e44be8.

Brown, Juanita, and David Isaacs. *The World Café: Shaping Our Futures through Conversations That Matter*. Oakland, CA: Berrett-Koehler, 2005.

Brueggemann, Walter. "Another Other Kingdom." *Restore Commons*, November 5, 2018. https://www.restorecommons.com/another-other -kingdom/.

———. *Journey to the Common Good*. 2010. Louisville, KY: Westminster John Knox Press, 2021.

———. *Out of Babylon*. Nashville, TN: Abingdon Press, 2010.

Butler, Mike. "Building a Healthy and Just Community." *Restore Commons*, May 4, 2012. https://www.restorecommons.com/building-a-healthy-and -just-community/.

———. "Ensuring Public Safety in a Sustainable Way." Restore Commons, August 6, 2019. https://www.restorecommons.com/ensuring-public -safety-in-a-sustainable-way/.

Cahn, Edgar S. *No More Throw-Away People: The Co-Production Imperative*. Washington, DC: Essential Books, 2004.

———. "What Is TimeBanking?" *Restore Commons*. https://www .restorecommons.com/what-is-time-banking/. Accessed May 21, 2021.

Chapin, Ross. "Making Space for Community." *Restore Commons*, June 16, 2015. https://www.restorecommons.com/making-space-for-community/.

Clark, Adam. "Visions of a Just Economy." *Restore Commons*, June 7, 2016. https://www.restorecommons.com/visions-of-a-just-economy/.

Conboy, Edd. "A Place at the Table." *Restore Commons*, August 27, 2015. https://www.restorecommons.com/a-place-at-the-table/.

Cooke, Sekou. "The Fifth Pillar: A Case for Hip-Hop Architecture." *Arch Daily*, April 30, 2014. https://www.archdaily.com/501449/the-fifth-pillar-a-case -for-hip-hop-architecture/.

———. *Hip-Hop Architecture*. London, UK: Bloomsbury, 2021.

Cornuelle, Richard. "Our One-Eyed Press." In *De-Managing America: The Final Revolution,* by Richard Cornuelle, 35–39. New York: Random House, 1976.

Crawford, Matthew. *Shop Class as Soulcraft: An Inquiry into the Value of Work*. New York: Penguin Books, 2010.

Dallas, Paloma, and Paula Ellis, eds. *Reinventing Journalism to Strengthen Democracy: Insights from Innovators*. Dayton, OH: Kettering Foundation, 2023.

Ellis, Paula. "New Ways to Tell the News." *Restore Commons*. December 6, 2018. https://www.restorecommons.com/new-ways-to-tell-the-news/.

Esteva, Gustavo, Salvatore Babones, and Philipp Babcicky. *The Future of Development: A Radical Manifesto*. Bristol, UK: Policy Press, 2013.

Frazier, Nishani. "A 'New Direction': Rediscovering Community Wealth Building in an Age of Gentrification." *The Next System Project*, November 9, 2021, 1–29. https://thenextsystem.org/learn/stories/new-direction -rediscovering-community-wealth-building-age-gentrification.

Gunja, Munira Z., Evan D. Gumas, and Reginald D. Williams II. "U.S. Health Care from a Global Perspective, 2022: Accelerating Spending, Worsening Outcomes." The Commonwealth Fund, Issue Briefs, January 31, 2023. https://www.commonwealthfund.org/publications/issue-briefs/2023/jan /us-health-care-global-perspective-2022#1.

Hardin, Garrett. "The Tragedy of the Commons." *Science* 162, no. 3859 (December 13, 1968): 1243–1248. https://pages.mtu.edu/~asmayer/rural _sustain/governance/Hardin%201968.pdf.

Harges, DeAmon. "The Neighborhood Is the Center." *Restore Commons*, August 4, 2020. https://www.restorecommons.com/the-neighborhood-is -the-center/.

"Harrison Owen on Open Space." 5 videos. *Restore Commons*. http://www .restorecommons.com/author/harrison-owen/.

Holman, Peggy. "An Open Letter to Journalists." *Restore Commons*, June 13, 2020. https://www.restorecommons.com/open-letter-to-journalists/.

Hyde, Bruce, and Drew Kopp. *Speaking Being: Werner Erhard, Martin Heidegger, and a New Possibility of Being Human.* Hoboken, NJ: Wiley, 2019.

Ivory, Gary. "Organizing Residents to Solve an Impossible Challenge." *Restore Commons*, February 1, 2019. https://www.restorecommons.com /organizing-residents-to-solve-an-impossible-challenge/.

Korten, David C. *Change the Story, Change the Future: A Living Economy for a Living Earth.* Oakland, CA: Berrett-Koehler, 2015.

Kovitch, Joseph. "Church Turned Inside Out." *Restore Commons*. https://www .restorecommons.com/church-turned-inside-out/. Accessed May 21, 2023.

Kretzmann, John P., and John McKnight. *Building Communities from the Inside Out: A Path toward Finding and Mobilizing a Community's Assets.*

Evanston, IL: Asset-Based Community Development Institute, Institute for Policy Research, Northwestern University, 1993.

Lane, Jodi, Nicole Rader, et al. *Fear of Crime in the United States: Causes, Consequences, and Contradictions.* Durham, NC: Carolina Academic Press, 2014.

Leibovitz, Liel. *A Broken Hallelujah: Rock and Roll, Redemption, and the Life of Leonard Cohen.* New York: W.W. Norton & Company, 2014.

Livingston, Ann. "Organizing the Un-organizables." *Restore Commons*, April 2, 2018. https://www.restorecommons.com/organizing-the -unorganizables/.

Lovins, L. Hunter, and Stewart Wallis, et al. *A Finer Future: Creating an Economy in Service to Life.* Gabriola Island, BC: New Society Publishers, 2018.

Loy, David R. *A Buddhist History of the West.* Albany: State University of New York Press, 2002.

——. "Religion of the Market." *Journal of the American Academy of Religion* 65, no. 2 (Summer 1997): 275–290. http://www.jonathantan.org/handouts /buddhism/Loy-Market.pdf.

Lupton, Robert D. *Toxic Charity: How Churches and Charities Hurt Those They Help, and How to Reverse It.* New York: HarperOne, 2011.

Lynch, Damon. "Becoming Joshua: A Path to Economic Freedom." *Restore Commons*, Winter, 2021.

——. "Rethinking Racism." *Restore Commons*, December 11, 2019. https:// www.restorecommons.com/rethinking-racism/.

Mather, Mike. "From Charity to Empowerment." *Restore Commons*. October 10, 2012. https://www.restorecommons.com/from-charity-to -empowerment/.

——. *Having Everything, Possessing Nothing: Finding Abundant Communities in Unexpected Places.* Grand Rapids, MI: Eerdsmans Publishing, 2018.

McAfee, Barbara. *Full Voice: The Art and Practice of Vocal Presence.* San Francisco, CA: Berrett-Koehler, 2011.

McKnight, John. *Associational Life: Democracy's Power Source*. Edited by
Paula Ellis and Wendy Willis. Dayton, OH: Kettering Foundation, 2022.

———. "A Compilation of John McKnight's Learnings." Tamarack Institute,
2019. https://johnmcknight.org/learnings.

———. "Neighborhood Necessities: Seven Functions That Only Effectively
Organized Neighborhoods Can Provide." *National Civic Review.* October
18, 2013. https://resources.depaul.edu/abcd-institute/publications
/publications-by-topic/Documents/Neighborhood%20Necessities
%202013.pdf.

McKnight, John, and Peter Block. *The Abundant Community: Awakening the
Power of Families and Neighborhoods*. San Francisco, CA: Berrett-Koehler,
2012.

Moyer, Bill. "The Four Roles of Social Activism." The Commons Social Change
Library. https://commonslibrary.org/the-four-roles-of-social-activism/.
Accessed May 22, 2023.

Moyer, Bill, JoAnn McAllister, Mary Lou Finley, and Steven Soifer. *Doing
Democracy: The MAP Model for Organizing Social Movements*. Gabriola
Island, BC: New Society Publishers, 2001.

Muller, Jerry Z. *The Mind and the Market: Capitalism in Modern European
Thought*. New York: Alfred A. Knopf, 2002.

Neal, Craig, Patricia Neal, and Cynthia Wold. *The Art of Convening: Authentic
Engagement in Meetings, Gatherings, and Conversations*. Oakland, CA:
Berrett-Koehler, 2011.

Owen, Harrison. *Open Space Technology: A User's Guide*. 3rd edition.
Oakland, CA: Berrett-Koehler, 2008.

Oxford English Dictionary Online. "common good." https://www.oed.com
/view/Entry/37228?redirectedFrom=common+good#eid.

Pascale, Richard, Jerry Sternin, and Monique Sternin. *The Power of Positive
Deviance: How Unlikely Innovators Solve the World's Toughest Problems*.
Boston: Harvard Business Press, 2010.

Patel, Raj. *The Value of Nothing: Why Everything Costs So Much More Than We
Think*. London: Granta Books, 2011.

Pearlman, Eve. "Dialogue Journalism: Adapting to Today's Civic Landscape." In *Reinventing Journalism to Strengthen Democracy: Insights from Innovators*, edited by Paloma Dallas and Paula Ellis. Dayton, OH: Kettering Foundation, 2023.

———. "Journalism with Community at the Center." *Restore Commons*, March 11, 2020. https://www.restorecommons.com/journalism-with -community-at-the-center/.

Pearlman, Eve, et al. "Dialogue Journalism Toolkit." *Spaceship Media* 18 (June 2019). https://spaceshipmedia.org/wp-content/uploads/2019/06/toolkit -526.pdf.

powell, john a. "Poverty and Race through a Belonginess Lens." *Policy Matters*, March 2012. https://www.law.berkeley.edu/files/PolicyMatters _powell_V4.pdf.

———. "Poverty Interrupted." *Neighborhood Partnerships*, April 2012. http://neighborhoodpartnerships.org/wp-content/uploads/2012/11 /PolicyMatters_johnpowell.pdf.

Puntenney, Deborah. "How Community Action Shapes Health." *Restore Commons*, June 6, 2017. https://www.restorecommons.com/how -community-action-shapes-health/.

Reed, Jackie. "Health Is a Neighborhood Issue." *Restore Commons*, September 9, 2014. http://www.restorecommons.com/health-is -a-neighborhood-issue/.

Rothstein, Richard. *The Color of Law: A Forgotten History of How Our Government Segregated America*. Illustrated edition. New York: Liveright Publishing, W.W. Norton & Company, 2017.

Rowe, Jonathan. *Our Common Wealth: The Hidden Economy That Makes Everything Else Work*. Oakland, CA: Berrett-Koehler, 2013.

Russell, Cormac, and John McKnight. *The Connected Community: Discovering the Health, Wealth, and Power of Neighborhoods*. Oakland, CA: Berrett-Koehler, 2022.

Sachs, Wolfgang, ed. *The Development Dictionary: A Guide to Knowledge as Power*. 2nd edition. London: Zed Books, 2009.

Sale, Kirkpatrick. *Rebels against the Future: The Luddites and Their War on the Industrial Revolution: Lessons for the Computer Age.* Cambridge, MA: Perseus Publishing, 1996.

Spinney, Margery. "Financing a New Housing Paradigm: Dividend Housing." *Restore Commons,* June 30, 2019. https://www.restorecommons.com /financing-a-new-housing-paradigm-dividend-housing/.

Symon, Robin. *Transformation: The Life and Legacy of Werner Erhard* (film), 2007. http://www.transformationfilm.com/transformation-the-life-and -legacy-of-werner-erhard/.

Terlinchamp, Miriam. "The Radical and Freeing Work of Enacting Jubilee." *Restore Commons.* https://www.restorecommons.com/radical-freeing -work-enacting-jubilee/. Accessed May 22, 2023.

Villanueva, Edgar. *Decolonizing Wealth: Indigenous Wisdom to Heal Divides and Restore Balance.* 2nd edition. Oakland, CA: Berrett-Koehler, 2021.

Walljasper, Jay, and Bill McKibben. *All That We Share: How to Save the Economy, the Environment, the Internet, Democracy, Our Communities and Everything Else That Belongs to All of Us.* Illustrated edition. New York: The New Press, 2010.

West, Cornel. *Keeping Faith: Philosophy and Race in America.* New York: Routledge, 1993.

Whitfield, Ed. "We Don't Need Butter, We Need the Cow or, Why Universal Basic Income Is Not the Solution We Think It Is." *Yes!,* December 10, 2018. https://www.yesmagazine.org/issue/good-money/2018/12/10/why -universal-basic-income-is-not-the-solution-we-think-it-is.

Wood, Ellen M. *The Origins of Capitalism: A Longer View.* Brooklyn, NY: Verso, 2002.

Yost, Jeff. "The Hometown of Your Dreams." *Restore Commons,* January 13, 2015. https://www.restecommons.com/the-hometown-of-your-dreams/.

Access Discussion Guides
and other resources at
www.restorecommons.com

Restore Commons

ACKNOWLEDGMENTS

My interest in the common good and well-being became serious when I ran across Mark Anielski. A spiritual economist, he opened an alternative world to me. Thank you, Mark. I also want to give a special thanks to the work of Gustavo Esteva and his colleagues. They exposed me to a whole other language from what I had always taken for granted about development, colonialism, and the measures of empire.

This book was given its original form when Deborah Costenbader gave order and summary to all the notes, quotes, reviews, and files that were sitting asleep somewhere in my hard drive. Thank you, Deborah, for the patience and grace you bring to assembling ideas.

Leslie Stephen is to blame for all of my writing over the past forty-plus years. She is much more dangerous than the editor-at-large job title she kneels behind. She understands the ideas better than I, and knows instantly which should be dropped and which are merely foolish and therefore worth pursuing.

This particular book was given first life by the support of Steve

Piersanti, founder and publisher emeritus of Berrett-Koehler Publishers. Every once in a while, he asks whether there is anything new worth publishing. Steve is amazing at reading the marketplace, is very helpful in providing editorial wisdom, and is courageous in his revolutionary spirit housed in what looks from a distance as a normal human being. He also begins each conversation with a silent prayer, which is always a welcome reminder in the midst of it all.

Thanks too to Jeevan Sivasubramaniam, managing director, editorial, at Berrett-Koehler. He holds the whole process together and is a perfect example of one who manages to serve the business and the people in a graceful, clear, and authentic way. I also want to thank the reviewers of an early manuscript: Britt Bravo, Robert Jensen, and Jill Swenson. They each invested in the well-being of the book, especially in aspects that were hard to decipher and painfully repetitious. Thanks to each for the honesty and care present in each comment.

The Berrett-Koehler production team makes the book happen and is a pleasure to work with. It is a partnership at every step, which is very welcome and needed. Katelyn Keating and David Peattie moved the production process along. Ashley Ingram brought her artistry in creating a cover and design that was attuned to my aesthetic and intention. Tanya Grove provided the interior design of the book. Praise is due for the open space and clean combination of type, spacing, flow, and more, which are all beautifully done. Amy Smith Bell was a gentle and very helpful copyeditor. Thanks also to Janet Reed Blake and Edward Wade for catching errors, omissions, and inconsistencies. It takes a special eye and patience to do this so well. Also credit to Leonard Rosenbaum for creating an index to make the book more accessible for the reader.

All of this matters in allowing the creation of a book to embody the same qualities that you want the book to have with its readers.

Maggie Rogers makes all my work function in the world. She is my reluctant interface with reality and has been trying to get me to set limits for years, with rare success.

Finally, I am grateful to family: Cathy, Heather, Grace, Jennifer, David, Ellen, Leyland, Jim, Virginie, and Auggie, all loving in their own way. And to friends: readers, partners, participants, podcasters, and social innovators who give me the encouragement to keep typing and talking, in the face of the constant inner voice that suggests perhaps I have said enough.

INDEX

Free-market consumer economy, 26–27. *See also* Capitalism
Free-market economy, 12, 42
Freedom vs. liberation, 40
Freire, Paulo, 9, 33

Gentrification, 50–52. *See also* Displacement
"Getting real," 3
Gifts, 42–44, 111
Goethe, Johann Wolfgang von, 52
Good life, defined, 36
Government vs. communal ownership, 40–41
Greater Rochester Health Foundation (GRHF), 133–134
Gross domestic product (GDP), 33–34

Harges, DeAmon, 125–126
Health, social determinants of, 133–134
Hearings for citizen involvement, 100
Hip-hop, a center for, 134–135
Hip-hop architecture, 90–91
Holman, Peggy, 80, 81
Hosting, the art of, 116–117
Housing. *See also* Cohousing
  dividend, 87–89

Imagination, xxii
Income, as measure of well-being, 33–34
Individualism, xiv, 35–36, 41
Industrial Revolution, 102
  and business perspective, 23
  enclosure and, 13–14, 23
  impact, 28–29
Intent, clarifying, 117
Interior design, 84
Invitation, 108, 117
Ivory, Gary, 128–129

Journalism, 69–70. *See also* News

citizen requests, 80–81
common good, 72–75
dialogue, 79–80
neighborhoods and, 123–124
new, 10
partnership between citizens and journalists, 80–81
power of, 69
that matters, 80–81
transforming, 80
view from the front office, 71–73
what journalists offer, 81
Jubilee (biblical), 56, 67
and a just economy, 56–57
"Just talk," 105–106
Justice, 75–76

Koestenbaum, Peter, 82
Kovitch, Joseph "Father Joe," 62, 66–67

Labels, misuse of, 13, 38–39, 46–48
Land. *See also* Ownership
  business perspective vs. common good narrative on, 83–84
  our, 48–50
Leader–follower relationship, 97, 98
Leadership
  is convening, 97–98
  traditional "strong," 97–98
Liberation, 9
  vs. freedom, 40
Livingston, Ann, 131, 132
Local actions, news focusing on, 77–80
Local activism, xii, xviii, 47, 73, 74
  examples, 125–136
Local businesses, 35, 123, 127
Local economies, 10, 19, 28, 34, 35, 60, 123
  Community Reinvestment Act (CRA) and, 51
  examples, 129–130
Local products, 35, 124

ABOUT THE AUTHOR

PETER BLOCK is an author and citizen of Cincinnati, Ohio. His work is about chosen accountability, the reconciliation of community, and reclaiming communal well-being.

He is the author of several bestselling books. The most widely known are *Flawless Consulting: A Guide to Getting Your Expertise Used* (1980, 2023); *Stewardship: Choosing Service over Self-Interest* (1993, 2013); *Community: The Structure of Belonging* (2008, 2018); *The Answer to How Is Yes: Acting on What Matters* (2002, 2003); and *The Empowered Manager: Positive Political Skills at Work* (1987, 2017). He joined with John McKnight to write *The Abundant Community: Awakening the Power of Families and Neighborhoods* (2010) and with Walter Brueggemann and John McKnight to write *An Other Kingdom: Departing the Consumer Culture* (2016). His newest books are *Confronting Our Freedom: Leading a Culture of Chosen Accountability and Belonging*, coauthored with Peter Koestenbaum (2023), and *The Flawless Consulting Fieldbook and Companion: A Guide to Understanding*

Your Expertise, coauthored with twenty-eight contributors (2001, 2024).

The intent of Peter's work is to bring change into the world through consent and connectedness rather than through mandate and force. His books are about ways to create workplaces and communities that work for all. They offer an alternative to the patriarchal beliefs that dominate our culture.

Peter is founder of Designed Learning, a training company that offers workshops designed to build the skills outlined in his books. He has served his local neighborhood council, and is director emeritus of Elementz, an urban arts center in Cincinnati. With other volunteers in Cincinnati, Peter began A Small Group, whose work is to create a new community narrative and to bring his work on civic engagement into being. Peter joined with Darin Petersen in launching the Common Good Collective. Currently Peter is a part of Common Good Alliance, a Cincinnati effort to create everyday African American wealth by people collectively owning communal land, coming together to create places of Black culture, and investing in and controlling housing, enterprise, and the arts in local neighborhoods.

Peter's office is in Mystic, Connecticut. You can visit his websites at peterblock.com, designedlearning.com, and restorecommons.com. He welcomes being contacted at pbi@att.net.

ḻ designedLearning®

Founded by Peter Block in 1980, Designed Learning was established to offer workshops based on the ideas in Peter's books including his most well-known, *Flawless Consulting: A Guide to Getting Your Expertise Used* and *Community: The Structure of Belonging*. Since then, the team at Designed Learning has delivered training to thousands of people in thirty-five countries and in five languages, internally for global companies, and in public open-enrollment workshops.

At Designed Learning our vision is to create workplaces and communities that work for the common good of all through conversations to consult, convene, and empower. We do so by believing in an alternative narrative that values individual choice, accountability, cocreation, and the power of invitation over mandate.

In partnering with our clients, we help develop new skills to engage teams, invite collaboration, overcome isolation, and deepen connection, especially in a virtual environment. We design structured learning experiences that awaken a sense of purpose to create organizations that people believe in and will thrive—individually and collectively. Through our highly experiential in-person and virtual workshops, consulting, and coaching, we invite opportunities to move toward a more human culture of relatedness and connection where people learn how to build trusting relationships, get their expertise used, feel a greater sense of belonging, and accept freedom as a pathway to accountability.

If you share our vision, we invite you to visit our website or e-mail us directly to explore the possibilities or to be added to our rapidly growing community of individuals who want to become architects of the world they want to live in.

Website: www.designedlearning.com

E-mail: info@designedlearning.com

Discussion Guides for *Activating the Common Good*

available at www.designedlearning.com

Dear reader,

Thank you for picking up this book and welcome to the worldwide BK community! You're joining a special group of people who have come together to create positive change in their lives, organizations, and communities.

What's BK all about?

Our mission is to connect people and ideas to create a world that works for all.

Why? Our communities, organizations, and lives get bogged down by old paradigms of self-interest, exclusion, hierarchy, and privilege. But we believe that can change. That's why we seek the leading experts on these challenges—and share their actionable ideas with you.

A welcome gift

To help you get started, we'd like to offer you a **free copy** of one of our bestselling ebooks:

www.bkconnection.com/welcome

When you claim your **free ebook**, you'll also be subscribed to our blog.

Our freshest insights

Access the best new tools and ideas for leaders at all levels on our blog at ideas.bkconnection.com.

Sincerely,

Your friends at Berrett-Koehler